6.00

What's for Dinner? serves up great soups

Ken's Soup Krazy

Ken Kostick

LIFe

as seen on
Life Network

Canadian Cataloguing in Publication Data

Kostick, Ken, 1954–

    Ken's soup krazy: What's for dinner? serves up great soups

Includes index.

ISBN 0-13-018183-8

1. Soups.   I. Title.   II. Title: What's for dinner? serves up great soups

TX757.K67 2000   641.8'13   C00-930130-5

© 2000 Ken Kostick

ISBN 0-13-018183-8

Editorial Director, Trade Division: Andrea Crozier
Acquisitions Editor: Nicole de Montbrun
Copy Editor: Shaun Oakey
Production Editor: Jodi Lewchuk
Cover and Interior Design: Mary Opper
Cartoons: Denis Gonzalez
Production Manager: Kathrine Pummell
Page Layout: Gail Ferreira Ng-A-Kien
Photographs: Lorella Zanetti

  2 3 4 5 KR 04 03 02 01 00

Printed and bound in Canada.

Visit the Prentice Hall Canada Web site! Send us your comments, browse our catalogues, and more. **www.phcanada.com.**

Prentice
Hall
Canada

A Pearson Company

To Jamie, Benny and Pearl,

For your love and support.

Contents

Acknowledgments   viii

Crazy for Soup   x

Stir Struck   xii

I'm Talking Stocks   1

The Crème de la Puree   10

A Hill of Beans   36

A Mess of Vegetables   50

Chill, Baby   70

Lighten Up   84

Soup for the Sole   102

Chicken and Turkey Deelight   124

The Beef, the Bacon and the Wee Lamb   144

Haute, Haute, Haute   164

Index   186

Dear Ken   193

About Ken, Pearl and Benny   194

Acknowledgments

The following friends and family members have helped to make this book possible—it's great to have such a supportive network of people around me who continue to laugh at my corny jokes. Thanks for your laughter and much more over the past few years.

Nicole de Montbrun—my editor and friend. It's always a pleasure talking to you. You have incredible vision and insight, thus making my job easier. Your company at my cabin is always welcome. Thank you for your lovely friendship (and you have the sexiest voice!).

Gill Humphreys—my next door neighbour and best friend. What can I say? You are the best and a joy to have around. You also love my food, which is a big plus. Those days when I deliver little food gifts at your kitchen door always lead to hours spent swapping stories and tips about our fabulous beauty products. God, we look good!

Donald Martin—thank you for your continued support and friendship, which I cherish. It still amazes me that one person can be so talented and have so many extraordinary experiences to relate. And now that you live in Los Angeles, I especially love your wacky La La Land stories.

Mary Jo—you leave me speechless! But I love your whacked-out sense of humour; you keep me in stitches. Your lovely son has brought out the mother in you, and I can honestly say that you and Dean make wonderful parents. I am impressed. (But it's hard finding a good nanny, eh?)

Robert Townsend—my friend and travel agent. Boy, have you saved me a lot of stress this year! Thank you for being undoubtedly the world's best travel agent.

Ted Loviscek—friend and comedian. Thank you for being so funny and for helping me write some of the material I use. You have a great comedic sensibility.

The Television Crew—well, we must have eaten and drunk our way across Canada on the "road shows." Everyone made this more-than-two-month trip one of my most pleasurable travelling experiences. You guys are the greatest. Thanks.

Prentice Hall Canada—thanks to everyone for the generous support of this book. It really makes an author feel good to have the backing of such an illustrious publisher.

The Friendly Kitchen Company—hey, guys! Thanks again for your support for *What's for Dinner?* And for the books we've done together. Thanks, again.

Alliance Atlantis—thank you, Barb, Eleanor and everyone in the Programming, Promotions and Marketing Departments.

My dearest friends Rob, Barry, Nancy, Doug, Channing, Brian, Jason, Anne, Steve, Pauline, Georgette and all my buddies at Lake Winnipeg—thank you, again.

Helen—my mom—and her new addition, Rocky. Thanks for all your support over the last year in the preparation of this book. Love you!

Crazy for Soup

I really am soup crazy! Of course, I love to cook any and every dish or entrée you can name, but I am passionate about soup.

Canadians love soup, too. I know this because each time I prepare a soup on *What's for Dinner?*, the show is deluged with letters from viewers asking for more. Well, here they are: herb-infused or cream-based, accented by pasta or rice and spiced up with chili, curry or cardamom. Many have appeared on the fifth season of the show, but many, many more are making their first appearance between these covers.

Soup is great for so many reasons. For instance, it's easy! Anyone can make a delicious soup (this I will prove, in the following pages). As well, it's extremely versatile: you can make hearty soups or light soups, hot soups or cool soups with whatever you have in the fridge or cupboard. It's also a wonderful way to use last night's leftovers, vegetables or meat. Lastly, not only is it healthy and often low in fat, but soup is also quick and economical—it can be a one-pot, one-dish meal, saving you time and money.

My parents, Helen and Ed Kostick, knew this well. Anytime the smell of chicken soup permeates my house it draws me back to those days in Winnipeg when I sat in the kitchen, watching Mom and Dad prepare soup—stock and all—from scratch. Although I've tried to make this cookbook as simple as possible for everyone, I couldn't walk away from it without also revealing how to get that same "from scratch" flavour.

With that in mind, I've begun *Ken's Soup Krazy* with the basics: chicken stock, beef stock, fish stock and vegetable stock, with variations and low-fat twists on the old standards. These can take time but are worth the effort. Of course, if you don't have the time, don't hesitate to buy the canned, low-sodium variety. Once you've got the stock, you can choose between nine chapters and every style of soup, including classic chunky chowders, minestrone or mulligatawny. There's also sections on creamed soups (The Crème de la Puree), vegetarian soups (A Mess of Vegetables), legumes soups (A Hill of Beans), low-fat soups (Lighten Up), chilled soups (Chill, Baby), chicken soups, meat soups, fish soups and devastatingly delicious (but not so economical) designer soups (Haute, Haute, Haute).

But before you pull out the stops, and that soup pot, keep in mind my philosophy: I've used creative license throughout, and so should you. Have fun and don't fret if you don't have all the ingredients. The recipes in this book are created in such a way that if you don't have oregano, you can use basil; if you don't want butter, you can use oil or leave it out entirely. Use your imagination and experiment; trust me, it won't go wrong. Substitute vegetables, greens, or anything. Try some of my variations (most of the recipes have at least one variation or low-fat option), or try your own and write to me (see the back of the book) to let me know how you fared.

Remember to always treat this cookbook as a handy guide, or a rough road map, to your very best *soup du jour*.

Stir Struck

Don't know where to begin? You needn't worry. The following is my handy, dandy guide to getting started and getting it right.

What you *absolutely* must have:
- A good, deep, soup pot, stock pot or Dutch oven
- A ladle
- A skimmer (to skim the fat)
- A slotted spoon
- A paring knife
- A grater or peeler
- A blender, hand blender or food processor

Basics you *should* have:
- Garlic cloves
- Bay leaves
- Salt and sea salt
- Black and white pepper
- Dried basil, oregano, sage, rosemary and thyme
- Chili powder and cayenne pepper
- Curry powder
- Ground nutmeg
- Soy sauce
- Worcestershire sauce
- Dijon mustard
- Olive oil
- Onions
- Carrots
- Milk, table cream and/or half-and-half

What you need to know:
- Simmer most soups; never boil unless I specifically instruct you to do so.
- If you don't have fresh vegetables, use frozen (frozen vegetables are preferable to canned).
- If your puree or chowder is too thick, add more broth, milk or cream.
- To make your own half-and-half, combine equal parts milk and light cream.
- When pureeing soup, do it in batches or, better yet, use a hand blender in the soup pot.
- Add salt to soup near or at the end of the cooking time.
- Add spices toward the beginning of the cooking process.
- Before freezing soup, cool it first, than place in a covered container, leaving 1/2 inch at the top for expansion room.
- 1 cup of dry beans or lentils is the equivalent of 3 1/2 cups of cooked or canned (and drained) beans or lentils.
- When garnishing, always use fresh herbs, not dried.

What you need to know when making stock:
- Stocks freeze well for up to 4–6 months.
- Once your stock is made, strain with a fine-meshed sieve or a sieve lined with cheesecloth.
- When making fish stock, use fish bones from fish such as cod, snapper, sole, grouper, monkfish or sea bass.
- Never use oily fish such as salmon for your base; my recipe for fish stock calls for using "non-oily" fish.
- If you prepare vegetable stock, avoid adding cabbage, turnips, or beets as these will discolour your stock and impart a too-pungent taste.

I'm Talking Stocks

Kenny's Chicken Stock   2

Low-Fat Chicken Stock   3

Chicken Broth with Ginger and Coriander   4

Beef Stock   5

Fish Stock   6

Kenny's Fancy Fish Stock   7

Vegetable Stock   8

Kenny's Special Vegetable Stock   9

Kenny's Chicken Stock

The trick to really good stock is patience!

Makes 12–14 cups

PER SERVING:
35 calories;
less than 1 g fat
(4% calories from fat);
2 g protein;
8 g carbohydrate;
0 mg cholesterol;
2429 mg sodium

1	5-lb chicken
1	large onion, quartered
1 tsp	sea salt
1 tsp	white pepper
16 cups	water
1	bay leaf

In a stock pot, combine the chicken, onion, salt, pepper, water and bay leaf. Bring to a boil, reduce heat and simmer, uncovered, 3 to 4 hours, without stirring. Strain the stock through a colander lined with cheesecloth. Pick all of the chicken meat from the bones and set aside to use later or freeze once cooled. Skim the fat from the top using a shallow spoon or paper towel. (You can put the pot into the fridge after the stock has cooled and let it sit 2 hours, then skim off the fat.) Allow to cool, then store in refrigerator for up to 2 days or freeze.

Variation
Add 1/2 cup white wine—it adds a very nice flavour.

Low-Fat Chicken Stock

This low-fat version is my preferred stock: you won't taste a big difference between this one and the non-low-fat chicken stock on the previous page.

Makes 12–14 cups

1	4- to 5-lb chicken, all skin and fat removed
1	large onion, quartered
4	cloves garlic, halved
1 tsp	dried basil
1 tsp	dried oregano
1 tsp	dried rosemary
1 tsp	sea salt
1 tsp	white pepper
16 cups	water
1	bay leaf

PER SERVING:

68 calories;

1 g fat

(9% calories from fat);

3 g protein;

15 g carbohydrate;

0 mg cholesterol;

2433 mg sodium

In a stock pot, combine the chicken, onion, garlic, basil, oregano, rosemary, salt, pepper, water and bay leaf. Bring to a boil, cover and simmer 3 to 4 hours, without stirring. Strain the stock through a colander lined with cheesecloth. Remove all of the chicken meat and set aside to use later or freeze once cooled. Skim the fat from the top using a shallow spoon or paper towel. (You can put the pot into the fridge after the stock has cooled and let it sit 2 hours, then skim off the fat.) Allow to cool, then store in refrigerator for up to 2 days or freeze.

Chicken Broth with Ginger and Coriander

*The soups I use with this stock always have an oriental flavour
and a combination of fresh herbs.*

Makes 12–14 cups

PER SERVING:

100 calories;

1 g fat

(6% calories from fat);

6 g protein;

20 g carbohydrate;

0 mg cholesterol;

4808 mg sodium

1	4- to 5-lb chicken
1	large onion, quartered
1/2 cup	fresh coriander sprigs
1/4 cup	soy sauce
1 tbsp	grated fresh ginger
1 tbsp	white pepper
1/2 tsp	sea salt
16 cups	water

In a stock pot, combine the chicken, onion, coriander, soy sauce, ginger, pepper, salt and water. Bring to a boil, reduce heat, cover and simmer 3 to 4 hours, without stirring. Strain the stock through a colander lined with cheesecloth. Pick all of the chicken meat from the bones and set aside to use later or freeze once cooled. Skim the fat from the top using a shallow spoon or paper towel. (You can put the pot into the fridge after the stock has cooled and let it sit 2 hours, then skim off the fat.) Allow to cool, then store in refrigerator for up to 2 days or freeze.

Beef Stock

Although this stock, like most, requires a lengthy time commitment, it's worth it. There's nothing better than a rich home-made beef stock as a base for soup or sauce.

Makes 12–14 cups

6 to 7 lb	beef bones, cracked
4	carrots, chopped into large pieces
4	stalks celery, chopped into large pieces
3	onions, quartered
3	parsnips, quartered
4	cloves garlic, halved
2	cloves
1 tsp	black pepper
1/2 tsp	sea salt
1/2 tsp	dried basil
1/2 tsp	dried thyme
1	bay leaf
16 cups	water

PER SERVING:

412 calories;

4 g fat

(9% calories from fat);

10 g protein;

94 g carbohydrate;

0 mg cholesterol;

2771 mg sodium

In a roasting pan, combine the beef bones, carrots, celery, onions, parsnips and garlic. Roast at 450°F for 15 minutes; turn the vegetables and roast for another 20 minutes. Place bones and vegetables in a stock pot and add cloves, pepper, salt, basil, thyme, bay leaf and water. Bring to a boil and remove the scum from the top. Reduce heat to a simmer. Pour 1 cup water into roasting pan and cook over medium-high heat, stirring to loosen any bits from the bottom of the pan. Pour into stock, cover and simmer about 4 hours, frequently removing scum from the top. Strain the stock through a colander lined with cheesecloth. Allow to cool, then store in refrigerator for up to 2 days or freeze.

Variation

For a richer flavour, add 1 cup red wine when you add the water.

Fish Stock

For most people, making a fish stock is much more intimidating than making a chicken stock; in fact, how to make a good fish stock is one of the most frequently asked questions thrown my way. Well, I hope the following recipe will have you hooked.

Makes 14 cups

PER SERVING:

79 calories;

1 g fat

(5% calories from fat);

3 g protein;

17 g carbohydrate;

0 mg cholesterol;

2154 mg sodium

6 lb	heads, skeletons and pieces from a non-oily fish*
2	large onions, quartered
2	cloves garlic, coarsely chopped
1 tsp	white pepper
1/2 tsp	sea salt
1/2 tsp	dried basil
1	bay leaf
16 cups	water

In a stock pot, combine the fish pieces, onions, garlic, pepper, salt, basil, bay leaf and water. Bring to a boil, cover and reduce heat to a simmer. Simmer 3 to 4 hours. Strain the stock through a colander lined with cheesecloth. Allow to cool, then store in refrigerator for up to 2 days or freeze.

*Avoid using salmon.

Variation
For a darker stock, add 1 cup red wine and 2 tbsp balsamic vinegar.

Kenny's Fancy Fish Stock

It's the wine and thyme that put the "fancy" in this fancy fish stock.

Makes 14 cups

6 lb	heads, skeletons and pieces from a non-oily fish[*]
2	large onions, quartered
2	leeks, cut into pieces
2	cloves garlic, halved
1/2 cup	chopped fresh basil
1/4 cup	chopped fresh thyme
1 tsp	white pepper
1/2 tsp	sea salt
1	bay leaf
1 cup	dry white wine
16 cups	water

PER SERVING:

442 calories;

4 g fat

(9% calories from fat);

12 g protein;

67 g carbohydrate;

0 mg cholesterol;

2209 mg sodium

In a stock pot, combine the fish pieces, onions, leeks, garlic, basil, thyme, pepper, salt, bay leaf, wine and water. Bring to a boil, cover, and reduce heat to a simmer. Simmer about 4 hours. Strain the stock through a colander lined with cheesecloth. Allow to cool, then store in refrigerator for up to 2 days or freeze.

[*]Avoid using salmon.

Vegetable Stock

*Vegetable stock is a permanent feature in my kitchen: I use it to sauté with,
in sauces and as a base for soup, again and again and again.*

Makes 14 cups

PER SERVING:
486 calories;
5 g fat
(7% calories from fat);
23 g protein;
108 g carbohydrate;
0 mg cholesterol;
1394 mg sodium

6	stalks celery with leaves, cut into pieces
6	carrots, chopped
4	large onions, skins on, quartered
3	leeks, sliced
6	cloves garlic, skins on, halved
4	tomatoes, chopped
1 cup	cauliflower florets
1 cup	broccoli florets
1/2 cup	chopped fresh parsley
1/4 cup	chopped fresh basil
1 tbsp	chopped thyme
1 tsp	pepper
1/2 tsp	sea salt
1	bay leaf
12 cups	water

In a stock pot, combine the celery, carrots, onions, leeks, garlic, tomatoes, cauliflower, broccoli, parsley, basil, thyme, pepper, salt, bay leaf and water. Bring to a
boil, cover and reduce heat to a simmer. Simmer about 2 hours, adding more
water if the stock evaporates too much. Strain the stock and allow to cool. Store
in refrigerator for up to 2 days or freeze.

Tip: After you strain out the vegetable mixture, discard the onion and garlic skins
and the bay leaf. Puree the vegetables and use later in sauces and soups.

Kenny's Special Vegetable Stock

This extremely easy to make vegetable stock was designed especially for you: make it and store it, but always keep it handy.

Makes 14 cups

PER SERVING:

415 calories;

3 g fat

(6% calories from fat);

15 g protein;

73 g carbohydrate;

0 mg cholesterol;

2930 mg sodium

5	carrots, chopped
4	large stalks celery with leaves, chopped
3	medium onions, quartered
3	leeks, sliced
4	cloves garlic, chopped
1/2 cup	chopped fresh parsley
1/2 tsp	dried basil
1/2 tsp	dried rosemary
1/2 tsp	dried thyme
1/2 tsp	sea salt
1/2 tsp	pepper
1	bay leaf
1/2 cup	dry white wine
12 cups	water

In a stock pot, combine the carrots, celery, onions, leeks, garlic, parsley, basil, rosemary, thyme, salt, pepper, bay leaf, wine and water. Bring to a boil, cover and reduce heat to a simmer. Simmer about 2 hours. Strain the stock. Allow to cool, then store in refrigerator for up to 2 days or freeze.

Variation

Puree the vegetables and add stock and cream to make a cream of vegetable soup.

The Crème de la Puree

Creamy Spinach Soup with Fennel   12

Sweet Potato Soup with Apple and Cinnamon   13

Sweet Potato Soup with Curry and Nutmeg   14

Curried Butternut Squash Soup   15

Pumpkin Curry Soup   16

Cauliflower and Mushroom Soup   17

Lentil and Tomato Soup   18

Carrot and Apple Soup with Ginger   19

Spicy Mushroom Soup with Cheese   20

Lots of Mushroom Soup   21

Cream of Mushroom Soup   22

Cream of Asparagus Soup with Roasted Garlic and Basil   23

Cream of Broccoli and Cheese Soup   24

Cream of Zucchini and Herb Soup   25

Cream of Zucchini Soup with Tarragon   26

Cream of Leek Soup with Chives and Sour Cream   27

Cream of Artichoke Soup   28

Cream of Corn and Potato Soup   29

Corn and Potato Chowder with Cheese   30

Corn Soup with Rosemary and Port   31

True Potato Soup with Parmesan   32

Potato and Leek Soup with White Wine and Tarragon   33

Spicy Red Pepper Soup with Fresh Parsley   34

Avocado and Fresh Mint Soup   35

Creamy Spinach Soup with Fennel

Spinach accompanied by fennel creates a wonderful taste sensation.
Be Popeye and impress your olive oil with this recipe.

Serves 6

2 tbsp	olive oil
1	medium onion, chopped
1 cup	spinach, chopped
2	medium potatoes, cubed
1	fennel bulb, chopped
6 cups	vegetable stock
1/2 tsp	dried basil
1/2 tsp	dried thyme
1/2 tsp	dried mint
1/2 tsp	dried oregano
1/2 tsp	black pepper
1/4 tsp	ground nutmeg
1	bay leaf
1 cup	table cream

Variation

Replace the fennel with 1 cup chopped celery. Replace the table cream with non-fat milk or skim milk.

In a large soup pot, heat the oil. Add the onion and sauté for 2 minutes. Add the spinach; reduce heat to a simmer. Add the potatoes, fennel and stock; simmer 4 minutes or until the vegetables are tender. Add the basil, thyme, mint, oregano, pepper, nutmeg and bay leaf. Simmer 10 minutes and discard bay leaf. Add the cream and using a hand blender, puree the soup until smooth. Serve immediately.

Tip: If the soup reduces too much during the simmer stage, just add more stock.

Sweet Potato Soup with Apple and Cinnamon

*The sweet potato is a root vegetable and not a member of the potato family.
This root vegetable is originally from South America but is now
widely grown throughout North America.*

Serves 8

8 cups	vegetable stock
1 cup	apple juice
1 cup	applesauce
3	medium sweet potatoes, peeled and cubed (about 4 cups)
2	potatoes, peeled and cubed
2	apples, peeled, cored and cubed
1	small onion, chopped
1 tbsp	lemon juice
1/2 tsp	dried basil
1/2 tsp	cinnamon
1/2 tsp	black pepper
1	bay leaf

In a large soup pot, combine the stock, apple juice and applesauce. Bring to a boil.
Add the sweet potatoes, potatoes, apples, onion, lemon juice, basil, cinnamon,
black pepper and bay leaf. Cook over medium heat for 10 minutes; reduce heat
and simmer another 10 minutes or until the sweet potatoes and potatoes are tender. Remove the bay leaf. Using a hand blender, puree the soup until smooth.
Serve hot.

Variation
Replace the sweet potato with yam.

Sweet Potato Soup with Curry and Nutmeg

I bet you never know what to do with sweet potatoes! Get to your soup station and try this one—you'll be thanking me later!

Serves 6

4 cups	sweet potatoes, chopped
1	19-oz can stewed tomatoes
1	medium onion, chopped
2 tbsp	brown sugar
1 tsp	mild curry powder
1/2 tsp	dried basil
1/2 tsp	black pepper
1/2 tsp	salt
1/4 tsp	ground nutmeg
1	bay leaf
8 cups	vegetable stock

In a large soup pot, combine the sweet potatoes, tomatoes and their juice, onion, sugar, curry powder, basil, pepper, salt, nutmeg, bay leaf and stock. Simmer for 20 minutes. If the stock reduces, just add more. Remove the bay leaf. Using a hand blender, puree the soup until smooth. Serve immediately.

Curried Butternut Squash Soup

Every time I serve this to guests they rave about the hint of curry:
it's like a quick trip to the Far East!

Serves 8

6 cups	vegetable stock
3 cups	chopped butternut squash
1	small onion, chopped
1	large potato, cubed
1	bay leaf
1 tsp	brown sugar
1 tsp	curry powder
1/2 tsp	dried basil
1/2 tsp	dried oregano
1/2 tsp	cinnamon
1/2 tsp	salt
1/2 tsp	black pepper
1/4 tsp	ground nutmeg
1 cup	table cream
1/4 cup	chopped fresh parsley

LowFatOption

Replace the table cream with low-fat soy milk or non-fat milk beverage. Replace the brown sugar with calorie-reduced liquid sweetener. Use low-fat vegetable stock. 52.5 cal.

In a large soup pot, bring the stock to a boil. Add the squash, onion, potato, bay leaf, sugar, curry powder, basil, oregano, cinnamon, salt, pepper and nutmeg. Continue boiling until the squash and potato are tender, about 30 minutes. Discard the bay leaf. Puree the soup with a hand blender or in a food processor. Gently fold in the cream and parsley and serve.

Pumpkin Curry Soup

You shouldn't have to wait for Halloween to enjoy your pumpkin.
Use a smaller pumpkin; they taste better.

Serves 6

2 tbsp	olive oil
1	medium onion, chopped
4 cups	pumpkin, chopped
1	clove garlic, chopped
2 tsp	brown sugar
2 tsp	mild curry powder
1/2 tsp	cinnamon
1/2 tsp	dried thyme
1/2 tsp	salt
1/2 tsp	black pepper
6 cups	vegetable stock
1/4 cup	chopped fresh coriander

In a large soup pot, heat the oil. Sauté the onion for 2 minutes. Add the pumpkin and garlic; sauté for another 2 to 3 minutes. Stir in the sugar, curry powder, cinnamon, thyme, salt, pepper and stock. Simmer 15 minutes or until the pumpkin is tender. Puree the soup with a hand blender or in a food processor until it is nice and smooth. Serve with fresh coriander as a garnish.

Cauliflower and Mushroom Soup

I always hated cauliflower as a kid; I was soooo misguided.
Try this, you'll love it.

Serves 6

4 cups	button mushrooms, chopped
2 cups	chopped cauliflower
1	medium onion, chopped
2	cloves garlic, finely chopped
1/2 cup	chopped fresh parsley
1/4 cup	chopped fresh basil OR 1/2 tsp dried
1 tbsp	chopped fresh rosemary OR 1/4 tsp dried
1/2 tsp	salt
1/2 tsp	black pepper
1	bay leaf
8 cups	vegetable stock
1/2 cup	grated Parmesan cheese

> ## Variation
> Replace the Parmesan with blue cheese.

In a large soup pot, combine the mushrooms, cauliflower, onion, garlic, half of the parsley, basil, rosemary, salt, pepper, bay leaf and stock. Bring to a boil; reduce heat and simmer 20 minutes. Remove the bay leaf. Using a hand blender, puree the soup until it has a smooth, creamy texture. Stir in the Parmesan cheese. Garnish with the remaining parsley.

Lentil and Tomato Soup

You'll be loving this lentil-tomato-Parmesan-sage-Dijon combination for lunch, dinner and any time in between. Sage brings out the flavour in most dishes.

Serves 8

2 cups	lentils
1	28-oz can crushed tomatoes
1	large plum tomato, chopped
1	small onion, chopped
2	cloves garlic, chopped
2 tbsp	Dijon mustard
1 tbsp	Worcestershire sauce
1/2 tsp	dried sage
l/2 tsp	dried oregano
1/2 tsp	salt
1/2 tsp	black pepper
1	bay leaf
1/2 cup	chopped fresh parsley
6 cups	low-sodium/low-fat vegetable stock
1/4 cup	grated Parmesan cheese

In a large soup pot, combine the lentils, crushed tomatoes, plum tomato, onion, garlic, mustard, Worcestershire sauce, sage, oregano, salt, pepper, bay leaf, half of the parsley and the stock. Bring to a boil. Reduce heat and simmer for 25 minutes. Discard the bay leaf. Using a hand blender, puree the soup until it is creamy. Serve immediately, garnished with the remaining parsley and the Parmesan cheese.

Carrot and Apple Soup with Ginger

*My mom (Helen K.) used to disguise carrots on the plate to fool me;
my immature and foolhardy taste buds have done a 180 degree turn since I
discovered the superb taste-bud-tingly combination of carrots, apple and ginger.*

Serves 6

1 tbsp	vegetable oil	1/4 cup	chopped fresh dill
1	medium onion, chopped	2 tbsp	finely chopped fresh ginger
2	cloves garlic, minced	1 tbsp	chopped fresh thyme
1/2	red bell pepper, chopped	1/2 tsp	chili powder
4 cups	coarsely chopped carrots	1/2 tsp	salt
2	apples, peeled, cored and chopped	1/2 tsp	black pepper
		1	bay leaf
1 cup	apple juice	6 cups	vegetable stock
1/4 cup	chopped fresh basil	1/2 cup	table cream (optional)

In a large soup pot, heat the oil. Add the onion and garlic and sauté for 2 minutes or until the onion is translucent. Add the red pepper and sauté for another 2 minutes. Add carrots, apples, apple juice, basil, dill, ginger, thyme, chili powder, salt, pepper, bay leaf and stock; bring to a boil. Reduce heat to medium and simmer, uncovered and stirring occasionally, for 20 minutes. Remove the bay leaf. Using a hand blender or food processor, puree the soup until smooth. For a creamier consistency, fold in cream at the very end.

Spicy Mushroom Soup with Cheese

*Hoochie mama! This is a scrumptious soup with a
surprise ending (a kicker, actually).*

Serves 8

LowFatOption

Use skim milk. Use
low-fat cheddar
cheese.
104.0 cal.

8 cups	low-sodium/low-fat vegetable stock
1 tsp	chili powder
1/2 tsp	dried oregano
1/2 tsp	dried thyme
1/2 tsp	paprika
1/2 tsp	salt
1/2 tsp	black pepper
1/4 tsp	cayenne pepper (optional)
5 cups	button mushrooms, chopped
3	medium potatoes, cubed
1	medium onion, chopped
2	cloves garlic, finely chopped
1	19-oz can stewed tomatoes
2 cups	milk
1/2 cup	shredded cheddar cheese

In a large soup pot, bring the stock to a boil. Add the chili powder, oregano, thyme, paprika, salt, pepper and cayenne. Cook, stirring, for 5 minutes. Add the mushrooms, potatoes, onion, garlic and stewed tomatoes and their juice. Simmer for 20 minutes or until the potatoes are completely cooked. Using a hand blender, puree the soup to a creamy texture; if the soup is too thick, add some more stock. Add the milk and cheese and stir well over low heat until heated through and cheese has melted.

Tip: Stir a little of this soup into leftover mashed potatoes.

Lots of Mushroom Soup

I adore mushrooms. (Does that make me a FUNGUY?)

Serves 6

8 cups	vegetable or beef stock
1/2 tsp	salt
1/2 tsp	black pepper
1/2 tsp	dried basil
1/2 tsp	crushed dried rosemary
1/4 tsp	dried thyme
6 cups	chopped assorted mushrooms
2	stalks celery, chopped
1	medium onion, chopped
2	potatoes, chopped
1	bay leaf
1 tbsp	Dijon mustard
1 cup	cream
1/4 cup	chopped fresh parsley

In a large soup pot, bring the stock, salt, pepper, basil, rosemary and thyme to a boil. Add the mushrooms, celery, onion, potatoes and bay leaf. Reduce heat, cover and simmer 20 minutes. Remove the bay leaf. Using a hand blender, puree the soup to a creamy consistency. Stir in the mustard and cream; simmer another 2 minutes or until heated through. Garnish with the parsley and serve hot.

Cream of Mushroom Soup

Mushroom soup was a Kostick family favourite when Kenny was a wee lad …
this creamy version is great big tall Kenny's chef-d'oeuvre.

Serves 6

1 tbsp	olive oil	1/4 tsp	salt
1	small onion, chopped	1/2 tsp	black pepper
2	cloves garlic, minced	1 tbsp	lemon juice
4 cups	finely chopped button mushrooms	4 cups	vegetable stock
		1 cup	milk
1/4 cup	chopped fresh parsley	1 cup	half-and-half cream
1/2 tsp	dried basil	1/2 cup	whipping cream
1/2 tsp	dried oregano		Fresh parsley or watercress

> ### Variation
> Use any type or combination of fresh mushrooms for added flavour.

In a large heavy soup pot, heat the oil. Sauté the onion and garlic until the onion is translucent. Add the mushrooms and sauté until browned. Add the parsley, basil, oregano, salt, pepper, lemon juice and stock. Bring to a boil; reduce heat and simmer for 15 minutes. Add the milk, half-and-half cream and whipping cream. Simmer gently until heated through. Serve garnished with parsley or watercress.

> ### Low**Fat**Option
> Replace whipping cream with low-fat sour cream. Replace milk with a non-fat milk beverage or skim milk.
> 243.8 cal.

Cream of Asparagus Soup with Roasted Garlic and Basil

When the sublime elegance of asparagus is embellished with robust roasted garlic and invigorated by fresh basil leaves, the taste will leave you gasping for superlatives—I promise!

Serves 6

15	cloves roasted garlic
2 tbsp	olive oil
4	shallots, chopped
12	asparagus spears, chopped
1	small red bell pepper, chopped
1/2 cup	finely chopped fresh basil
1/4 cup	dry white wine
1/2 tsp	dried thyme
6 cups	low-fat vegetable stock
1 cup	skim milk

To roast garlic, peel the 15 cloves and place under broiler for 8–10 minutes until golden. Allow to cool. In a large soup pot, heat the oil. Add the shallots, asparagus and red pepper; sauté 4 minutes or until asparagus is tender. Add the roasted garlic, half of the basil, the wine and thyme. Allow to reduce, 4 to 5 minutes. Add the stock and bring to a boil. Reduce heat and simmer for 15 minutes. Using a hand blender, puree the soup until smooth. Stir in the milk; simmer gently until heated through. Stir in remaining basil and serve immediately.

Tip: Roast 30–40 cloves of garlic and store in the refrigerator for up to 7 days for other recipes.

Cream of Broccoli and Cheese Soup

Eat your broccoli! But do it with cheddar.

Serves 6

6 cups	vegetable stock
4 cups	broccoli florets
1	small onion, chopped
2	cloves garlic, chopped
1/2 tsp	dried basil
1/2 tsp	dried oregano
1/2 tsp	dried thyme
1/2 tsp	salt
1/2 tsp	black pepper
1 cup	milk
1/2 cup	table cream
3/4 cup	shredded cheddar cheese
1/4 cup	chopped fresh chives

Variation
Replace the broccoli with cauliflower.

In a large soup pot, bring the stock to a boil; reduce heat to a simmer. Add the broccoli, onion, garlic, basil, oregano, thyme, salt and pepper. Simmer 15 minutes or until broccoli is cooked. Using a hand blender, puree the soup until smooth. Stir in the milk, cream and cheese; simmer gently until the cheese melts, stirring to ensure it does not stick to the bottom of the pot. If the soup is too thick, add some more stock or milk. Garnish with chives and serve.

LowFatOption
Use skim milk. Replace the cream with non-fat sour cream. Use low-fat cheddar cheese. Use low-fat vegetable stock.
117.3 cal.

Cream of Zucchini and Herb Soup

*If you were ever under the mistaken impression that zucchini is a
flavourless vegetable, you've got to try this soup.*

Serves 8

2 tbsp	olive oil
1	medium onion, chopped
1	clove garlic, chopped
6	medium zucchini, cubed
2	small potatoes, cubed
1	red bell pepper, chopped
1 tbsp	dried parsley OR 1/2 cup chopped fresh
1/2 tsp	dried basil
1/2 tsp	dried oregano
1/2 tsp	dried thyme
1/2 tsp	black pepper
1	bay leaf
6 cups	vegetable stock
1/4 cup	dry white wine
2 cups	milk
1/2 cup	table cream

LowFatOption

Use 1/4 cup vegetable
stock to sauté instead
of olive oil. Replace
the milk with skim
milk and the cream
with non-fat sour
cream. Use low-fat
vegetable stock.
208.6 cal.

In a large non-stick soup pot, heat the oil. Sauté the onion and garlic for 2 minutes or until the onion is translucent. Add the zucchini, potatoes, red pepper, parsley, basil, oregano, thyme, pepper, bay leaf, stock and wine. Bring to a boil; reduce heat and simmer 15 minutes or until zucchini and potatoes are cooked. Add the milk and cream; simmer another 5 minutes. If the soup is too thick, add some more stock or milk. Remove the bay leaf. Using a hand blender, puree the soup and serve immediately.

Cream of Zucchini Soup with Tarragon

I had a version of this soup at my favourite restaurant: Jane and Paula's!

Serves 4 to 6

3 tbsp	olive oil
1	small onion, chopped
2	cloves garlic, finely chopped
3 cups	cubed zucchini
1	red bell pepper, chopped
5 cups	chicken stock
1/4 cup	finely chopped fresh tarragon
1 tbsp	Dijon mustard
1 tbsp	balsamic vinegar
1/2 tsp	dried basil
1/2 tsp	salt
1/2 tsp	white pepper
1 cup	table cream
	Fresh tarragon sprigs

In a large soup pot, heat the oil. Add the onion and garlic; sauté for 2 minutes or until the onion is translucent. Add the zucchini and red pepper and sauté another 2 minutes. Add the stock, tarragon, mustard, balsamic vinegar, basil, salt and pepper. Simmer 10 minutes; be careful not to overcook the zucchini. Stir in the cream and heat another 2 minutes or until heated through. Serve immediately garnished with a couple of sprigs of fresh tarragon.

Cream of Leek Soup with Chives and Sour Cream

Leek mingled with herbs and chives makes for a great soup.

Serves 6

3 tbsp	olive oil
3 cups	leeks, cut into pieces
2	cloves garlic, finely chopped
1/2 cup	grated carrot
1/2 cup	finely chopped fresh chives
1/2 tsp	dried basil
1/2 tsp	dried thyme
1/2 tsp	dried oregano
1/2 tsp	salt
1/2 tsp	black pepper
5 cups	vegetable stock
1 cup	table cream
1/4 cup	sour cream

LowFatOption

Replace olive oil with canola oil. Use low-fat vegetable stock. Replace cream with skim milk. Use non-fat sour cream. 115.8 cal.

In a large soup pot, heat the oil. Add the leeks and sauté for 2 minutes or until tender. Add the garlic and sauté another minute. Add the carrot, half of the chives, basil, thyme, oregano, salt, pepper and stock. Bring to a boil; reduce heat and simmer for 15 minutes. Add the table cream and stir well. Simmer until heated through. Serve with a dollop of sour cream and the remaining chopped chives on top.

Cream of Artichoke Soup

Chances are you haven't tried this one before! Well, give it a swirl.

Serves 4 to 6

1	medium onion, chopped
1	large potato, peeled and cubed
2 cups	sliced fresh artichokes
1/4 cup	finely chopped fresh parsley
1 tbsp	chopped fresh basil OR 1/4 tsp dried
1/2 tsp	salt
1/2 tsp	black pepper
5 cups	vegetable or chicken stock
1/2 cup	milk
1/2 cup	table cream

In a large soup pot, combine the onion, potato, artichokes, half of the parsley, basil, salt, pepper and stock. Simmer 20 minutes or until the artichokes and potato are cooked. Using a hand mixer, blend well. Stir in the milk and cream; simmer until heated through. Serve garnished with the remaining parsley.

LowFatOption

Use low-fat stock. Use skim milk. Replace table cream with low-fat sour cream.
62.3 cal.

Cream of Corn and Potato Soup

*This southern-accented soup will get your cowboy boots
in gear and your giddy-up!*

Serves 8

6 cups	vegetable stock
3 cups	thawed frozen or canned corn
2	large potatoes, peeled and cubed
1	small onion, chopped
1	clove garlic, chopped
2 tbsp	Dijon mustard
1/2 tsp	dried basil
1/2 tsp	dried thyme
1/2 tsp	salt
1/2 tsp	white pepper
1 cup	milk
1 cup	cream

Variation

Replace potatoes
with sweet potatoes
and add 1/2 tsp
cinnamon.

In a large soup pot, bring the stock to a boil; reduce heat to a simmer. Stir in the corn, potatoes, onion, garlic, mustard, basil, thyme, salt and pepper. Simmer 20 minutes or until the potatoes are cooked. Using a hand blender, blend the soup until smooth. (It's okay to have some whole corn kernels.) Stir in the milk and cream; simmer another 5 minutes or until heated through.

LowFatOption
Use skim milk. Replace the cream with non-fat sour cream. Use low-fat vegetable stock.
124.4 cal.

Corn and Potato Chowder with Cheese

My neighbour Perry makes this soup quite often for his family. On the nights he does, they usually give thanks before and *after the meal!*

Serves 8

LowFatOption
Replace the olive oil with 1/4 cup vegetable stock to sauté. Replace the cheddar and Parmesan with low-fat versions. 275.2 cal.

2 tbsp	olive oil
1	medium onion, diced
2	cloves garlic, chopped
1	red bell pepper, diced
4	medium potatoes, boiled
6 cups	vegetable stock
2 cups	thawed frozen or canned corn
1/2 tsp	dried basil
1/2 tsp	dried oregano
1/2 tsp	black pepper
1/2 tsp	salt
2 cups	milk
1/2 cup	shredded cheddar cheese
1/4 cup	grated Parmesan cheese
1/4 cup	chopped fresh parsley

In a large soup pot, heat the oil. Sauté the onion, garlic and red pepper until onion is translucent. Add the potatoes and stock. Simmer for 15 minutes or until potatoes are cooked. Using a hand blender, puree the soup to a creamy texture. Add the corn, basil, oregano, black pepper and salt; simmer for 10 minutes. Add the milk, cheddar cheese and Parmesan cheese. Cook another 5 minutes until the chowder has a nice milky texture. Serve sprinkled with parsley.

Corn Soup with Rosemary and Port

I regularly sit down with Rosemary, tipple with Port and garnish with a farmer's wages worth of parsley: it's a great corn-soup tradition.

Serves 6 to 8

2 cups	thawed frozen or canned corn
6 cups	chicken stock
1 tbsp	chopped fresh rosemary OR 1/4 tsp dried
1 tbsp	Dijon mustard
1 tbsp	Port
1/2 tsp	salt
1 tsp	white pepper
1/2 cup	table cream (optional)
1/4 cup	chopped fresh parsley

Variation
Replace Port with dry sherry.

In a bowl and using a hand blender, puree the corn, 2 cups of the stock, rosemary and mustard until all large kernels are gone. In a large soup pot, heat the remaining stock. Add the corn mixture and bring to a boil; immediately reduce the heat and simmer for 10 minutes. Add the Port, salt and pepper; simmer another 5 minutes. Add the cream and mix gently another 2 minutes or until heated through. Serve immediately, garnished with the parsley.

LowFatOption
Use low-fat chicken stock. Replace the cream with low-fat sour cream or leave it out altogether.
70.4 cal.

True Potato Soup with Parmesan

*Talk about easy and great ... serve these spuds and
wow your friends and family.*

Serves 4 to 6

LowFatOption

Replace the olive oil
with canola oil. Use
low-fat vegetable
stock. Use low-fat
Parmesan cheese.
Leave out the sour
cream or use low-fat
sour cream.
170.4 cal.

2 tbsp	olive oil
1	medium onion, chopped
2	cloves garlic, chopped
5	potatoes, peeled and cubed
6 cups	vegetable stock
1/2 tsp	dried basil
1/2 tsp	dried thyme
1/2 tsp	salt
1/2 tsp	black pepper
1/2 cup	grated Parmesan cheese
1/4 cup	chopped fresh parsley
1/2 cup	sour cream

In a large soup pot, heat the oil. Add the onion and garlic; sauté for 2 minutes or
until the onion is translucent. Add the potatoes; sauté, stirring to keep potatoes
from sticking to the bottom. Add the stock, basil, thyme, salt and pepper; simmer
15 minutes. Using a hand blender, puree the soup. Stir in the Parmesan and parsley. Place a tablespoon of sour cream on each serving. Serve immediately.

Potato and Leek Soup with White Wine and Tarragon

Every Tom, Dick and Mary has his or her potato and leek version to impress you with. But wait till you try this one; it's leeks ahead!

Serves 8

1	large leek, cut in pieces
4	large potatoes, peeled and cubed
1	large onion, chopped
2	cloves garlic, chopped (optional)
1 tsp	dried tarragon OR 1/2 cup chopped fresh
1/2 tsp	dried basil
1/2 tsp	dried oregano
1/2 tsp	salt
1/2 tsp	black pepper
1	bay leaf
7 cups	vegetable stock
1/2 cup	dry white wine
1/2 cup	milk
1/2 cup	table cream
1/4 cup	chopped fresh parsley

LowFatOption

Replace milk and cream with skim milk. Use low-fat vegetable stock.
71.5 cal.

In a large soup pot, combine the leek, potatoes, onion, garlic, tarragon, basil, oregano, salt, pepper, bay leaf and stock. Simmer 15 minutes or until potatoes are cooked. Add the wine; simmer another 5 minutes. Remove the bay leaf. Using a hand blender, puree the soup until smooth. Stir in the milk and cream. Garnish with parsley and serve.

Spicy Red Pepper Soup with Fresh Parsley

Wow! Sweet and spicy peppers in a pot.

Serves 6

2 tbsp	olive oil
1	small onion, chopped
2	cloves garlic, finely chopped
4	large red bell peppers, chopped
6 cups	vegetable stock
1 cup	tomato juice
1/2 tsp	chopped jalapeno pepper OR 1/4 tsp cayenne pepper
1/2 tsp	salt
1/2 tsp	black pepper
1/2 cup	chopped fresh parsley

In a large soup pot, heat the oil. Add the onion, garlic and red peppers; sauté for 5 minutes or until the peppers are tender. Add the stock, tomato juice, jalapeno pepper, salt, black pepper and half of the parsley. Simmer 10 minutes. Using a hand blender, puree the soup until nice and smooth. Garnish with the remaining parsley and serve immediately.

Avocado and Fresh Mint Soup

This rich and flavourful soup will make you swoon.

Serves 6

3	large avocados, mashed
5 cups	vegetable stock
1/2 cup	table cream
1/4 cup	chopped fresh mint
1/4 cup	chopped fresh parsley
1/2 tsp	salt
1/2 tsp	black pepper

In a large soup pot, bring to a boil the mashed avocados and stock. Reduce heat and simmer for 10 minutes. Using a hand blender, puree the avocado until smooth. Add the cream, mint, parsley, salt and pepper; simmer another 5 minutes. Serve hot.

Low**Fat**Option
Use low-fat vegetable stock. Replace cream with skim milk.
134.4 cal.

A Hill of Beans

Vegetable Bean Soup with a Load of Basil   38

Creamy Mixed Bean Soup   39

Mixed Bean Shrimp and Salsa Soup   40

Spicy Mixed Bean Potato Puree with Cheddar Cheese   41

Spicy Tomato White Bean Soup with Red Wine   42

White Bean and Chick Pea Puree   43

White Bean Soup with Potato and Bacon   44

Red Bean, Mushroom and Chili Soup   45

Kidney Bean Soup with Cheddar and Ham   46

Red Bean Soup with Sausage   47

Spicy Black Bean Soup   48

Black Bean Salsa Soup with Corn   49

Vegetable Bean Soup with a Load of Basil

It's the loads of basil and, of course, the cup of red wine that make this bean and veggie baby worth trying.

Serves 6

Variation

Add 2 sliced grilled mild sausages.

6 cups	vegetable stock	1	19-oz can stewed tomatoes
1 cup	red wine	1/2 cup	chopped fresh basil
1	medium potato, cubed	1 tsp	chili powder
1	small zucchini, diced (about 1/2 cup)	1/2 tsp	dried thyme
		1/2 tsp	black pepper
1	medium onion, chopped	1/2 tsp	salt
2	cloves garlic, chopped	1/2 cup	cooked red kidney beans
1/2	green bell pepper, chopped	1/2 cup	cooked black beans
1/2	red bell pepper, chopped	1/4 cup	finely chopped fresh parsley

In a large soup pot, bring stock and wine to a boil; reduce heat to a simmer. Add the potato, zucchini, onion, garlic, green and red peppers, tomatoes and their juice, basil, chili powder, thyme, black pepper and salt. Simmer 15 minutes or until the vegetables are tender. Add the red and black beans and simmer another 5 minutes. Garnish with parsley and serve.

LowFatOption

Use low-fat vegetable stock.
192.0 cal.

Creamy Mixed Bean Soup

*Just as a reminder (bean there, done that!), beans are a terrific
source of potassium, iron, protein and vitamin B.*

Serves 6

2 tbsp	olive oil
2	stalks celery, chopped
1	green bell pepper, chopped
1	medium onion, chopped
2	cloves garlic, chopped
1 cup	stewed tomatoes, diced
1/4 cup	chopped fresh basil
1 tsp	chili powder
1/2 tsp	sea salt
1/2 tsp	black pepper
5 cups	vegetable stock
1 cup	cooked red kidney beans
1/2 cup	cooked white beans
1/2 cup	cooked black beans
1 cup	table cream

In a large soup pot, heat the oil. Add celery, green pepper, onion and garlic; sauté
for 3 minutes or until the onion is translucent. Add the tomatoes and their juice,
basil, chili powder, salt, black pepper and stock. Bring to a boil; reduce heat and
simmer for 10 minutes. Add the red, white and black beans; simmer another 5
minutes. Add the table cream and simmer another 2 minutes or until heated
through. Serve immediately.

Mixed Bean Shrimp and Salsa Soup

*Although this recipe calls for a mild salsa, go wild
and choose hot if you want to.*

Serves 6

Variation

Replace the shrimp
with 2 cups cleaned,
rinsed clams.

2	stalks celery, chopped
1	medium red onion, chopped
1	small green bell pepper, chopped
1 cup	mild salsa
1 cup	cooked red kidney beans
1/2 cup	cooked white beans
1/2 cup	cooked black beans or chick peas
1 tbsp	lemon juice
1/2 tsp	dried basil
1/2 tsp	chili powder
1/2 tsp	salt
1/2 tsp	black pepper
7 cups	vegetable stock
1/2 cup	red wine
1 1/2 cups	cooked baby salad shrimp
1/4 cup	chopped fresh coriander

In a large soup pot, combine the celery, onion, green pepper, salsa, red, white and
black beans, lemon juice, basil, chili powder, salt, black pepper, stock and wine.
Bring to a boil; reduce heat and simmer for 15 minutes. Add the shrimp; simmer
gently until heated through. Stir in the coriander. Serve immediately.

Spicy Mixed Bean Potato Puree with Cheddar Cheese

Red beans, white beans and black beans with a dash of hot pepper and a sprinkling of cheese are an irresistible soup medley.

Serves 6 to 8

2 tbsp	olive oil		1/2 tsp	dried thyme
1	medium onion, chopped		1/2 tsp	hot pepper flakes
2	cloves garlic, chopped		1	bay leaf
2	potatoes, peeled and cubed		6 cups	vegetable stock
1/2 cup	cooked red kidney beans		1 cup	table cream
1/2 cup	cooked white beans		1/2 cup	shredded cheddar cheese
1/2 cup	cooked black beans		1/2 cup	chopped fresh parsley
1/2 tsp	dried oregano			

Variation

Replace the cheddar cheese with stilton or blue cheese for a richer, sharp taste.

In a large soup pot, heat the oil. Add the onion and garlic; sauté 2 to 3 minutes or until onion is translucent. Add potatoes, red, white and black beans, oregano, thyme, hot pepper flakes, bay leaf and stock. Bring to a boil; reduce heat and simmer 15 minutes or until potatoes are cooked. Remove the bay leaf. Using a hand blender, blend the soup until smooth. Add the cream and cheese. Simmer another 2 to 3 minutes to heat through. Stir in the parsley and serve immediately.

LowFatOption

Replace the cheddar cheese with a cheddar-flavoured soy or rice cheese.

Spicy Tomato White Bean Soup with Red Wine

Tomatoes, red wine and white beans is one of the most exciting combinations in this section.

Serves 6

Variation

Add 1 cup chopped cooked or leftover chicken or turkey.

1	28-oz can stewed tomatoes, diced
1 1/2 cups	cooked white beans
1/4 cup	chopped fresh basil
1 tbsp	chopped fresh oregano
1 tbsp	chopped fresh thyme
1/2 tsp	hot pepper flakes
1/2 tsp	sea salt
1/2 tsp	black pepper
1	bay leaf
6 cups	vegetable stock
1/2 cup	red wine
1/4 cup	chopped fresh parsley

In a large soup pot, combine the tomatoes and their juice, white beans, basil, oregano, thyme, hot pepper flakes, salt, pepper, bay leaf, stock and wine. Bring to a boil; reduce heat and simmer for 15 minutes. Remove the bay leaf. Garnish with parsley and serve.

White Bean and Chick Pea Puree

*This recipe is a stand-out. Serve it with a mesclun
salad and focaccia for a fabulous meal.*

Serves 6

1 1/2 cups	cooked chick peas
1 cup	cooked white beans
1	medium onion, chopped
1	small red bell pepper, chopped
1 tbsp	Dijon mustard
1 tsp	chili powder
1/2 tsp	dried basil
1/2 tsp	dried oregano
1/2 tsp	sea salt
1/2 tsp	black pepper
5 cups	vegetable stock
1 cup	table cream

In a large soup pot, combine chick peas, white beans, onion, red pepper, mustard, chili powder, basil, oregano, salt, black pepper and stock. Bring to a boil; reduce heat and simmer 15 minutes. Using a hand blender, blend the soup till smooth. Add the cream and simmer another 2 minutes or until heated through. Serve immediately.

LowFatOption
Replace the table cream with skim milk or soy milk.

White Bean Soup with Potato and Bacon

This soup is exceptionally delicious; you can always replace the bacon with lower-fat chicken or turkey bacon, but try the original recipe at least once.

Serves 6 to 8

1/2 lb	bacon, chopped
2 tbsp	olive oil
2	stalks celery, chopped
1	large red onion, chopped
1	red bell pepper, chopped
2	cloves garlic, chopped
1	medium potato, cubed
2	15-oz cans white beans (or 4 cups cooked beans)
1/2 cup	dry white wine
1/2 tsp	dried basil
1/2 tsp	dried thyme
1/2 tsp	salt
1/2 tsp	white pepper
1	bay leaf
8 cups	vegetable or chicken stock
1/4 cup	chopped fresh parsley

> **Variation**
>
> Replace bacon with turkey bacon or with 2 sliced grilled sausages.

In a large soup pot, fry the bacon until cooked but not crispy; drain on a paper towel. Drain the bacon fat from the pot. In the same pot, heat the oil; sauté the celery, onion, red pepper and garlic for 3 minutes. Add the potato and sauté another minute. Stir in the bacon, white beans and white wine; simmer until wine is reduced by half. Add the basil, thyme, salt, pepper, bay leaf and stock. Bring to a boil; reduce heat and simmer 15 minutes. Remove bay leaf and serve garnished with parsley.

Red Bean, Mushroom and Chili Soup

This soup is hot, hot, hot!

Serves 6

7 cups	vegetable stock
2 cups	chopped button mushrooms
1 cup	cooked red beans
1 cup	mild salsa
2	stalks celery, chopped
2	carrots, grated
1	medium onion, chopped
1/2 cup	red wine
1 tbsp	chili powder
1/2 tsp	dried basil
1/2 tsp	sea salt
1/2 tsp	black pepper
1	bay leaf
1/4 cup	chopped fresh parsley

In a large soup pot, bring the stock to a boil; reduce to a simmer. Add the mushrooms, red beans, salsa, celery, carrots, onion, wine, chili powder, basil, salt, pepper and bay leaf. Simmer for 15 minutes. Remove the bay leaf. Garnish with parsley and serve.

Variation

Replace the chili powder with mild curry powder. Replace the parsley with fresh coriander.

Kidney Bean Soup with Cheddar and Ham

*Cheddar and ham are inspired additions to kidney bean soup.
Enjoy this with hunks of home-made bread.*

Serves 6 to 8

2 tbsp	olive oil	1/2 cup	red wine
1	medium onion, chopped	1 cup	cubed cooked ham
1	green bell pepper, chopped	1/2 cup	chopped fresh coriander
1	medium carrot, grated	1 tsp	chili powder
4	cloves garlic, chopped	1/2 tsp	dried basil
2	15-oz cans kidney beans (or 4 cups cooked beans)	1/2 tsp	dried rosemary
2	medium potatoes, peeled and cubed	1/2 tsp	salt
2	medium tomatoes, chopped	1/2 tsp	black pepper
		1	bay leaf
		8 cups	vegetable or chicken stock
		1/2 cup	shredded cheddar cheese

In a large soup pot, heat the oil. Add the onion, green pepper, carrot and garlic; sauté for 2 minutes. Add the beans, potatoes, tomatoes and wine; allow to reduce slightly. Add the ham, coriander, chili powder, basil, rosemary, salt, black pepper, bay leaf and stock. Bring to a boil; reduce heat and simmer for 15 minutes. Remove the bay leaf. Garnish with cheese and serve immediately.

Red Bean Soup with Sausage

This red bean sausage soup is a complete—and healthy—meal.

Serves 4

1 cup	cooked red kidney beans
1	green bell pepper, chopped
1	red bell pepper, chopped
2	plum tomatoes, chopped
1	small onion, chopped
2	cloves garlic, chopped
1 tsp	chili powder
1/2 tsp	dried basil
1/2 tsp	dried oregano
1/2 tsp	black pepper
1/2 tsp	salt
5 cups	chicken stock
2	large beef, turkey or chicken sausages, grilled or baked, cut into pieces
1/4 cup	finely chopped fresh coriander or parsley

> ## Low**FatOption**
> Use low-fat chicken stock.
> 269.1 cal.

In a large soup pot, combine the beans, green and red peppers, tomatoes, onion, garlic, chili powder, basil, oregano, black pepper, salt and stock. Bring to a boil; reduce heat and simmer 10 minutes. Add the sausage and simmer another 5 minutes. Serve with chopped coriander or parsley.

Spicy Black Bean Soup

*This soup is heavenly. If you don't have sherry, no matter
(but you can always use dry wine instead).*

Serves 8

2 tbsp	olive oil
1	small onion, finely chopped
2	cloves garlic, finely chopped
1 tsp	seeded and finely chopped jalapeno pepper
1/2 tsp	ground oregano
1/2 tsp	dried basil
1	bay leaf
4 cups	cooked black beans
6 cups	vegetable stock
2 tbsp	dry sherry (optional)
1/2 tsp	sea salt
1/2 tsp	black pepper

In a large soup pot, heat the olive oil. Add the onion, garlic, jalapeno pepper, oregano, basil and bay leaf. Cook, stirring, until the onion is slightly golden. Stir in the beans and stock. Bring to a boil, stirring frequently to prevent beans from sticking to the bottom of the pot. As the soup begins to boil, slowly stir in the sherry. Add salt and pepper, stir well and serve.

LowFatOption

Replace the olive oil with a vegetable oil lower in saturated fats or calories.
Use low-fat vegetable stock.
376.6 cal.

Black Bean Salsa Soup with Corn

This Mexican-inspired soup is great served with tortillas and margaritas.

Serves 6

1 tbsp	olive oil	1/2 tsp	black pepper
2	stalks celery, chopped	1	bay leaf
1	medium onion, chopped	6 cups	vegetable stock
2	cloves garlic, minced	2 cups	cooked black beans
1 cup	mild or hot salsa	1/2 cup	cooked corn
1/4 cup	chopped fresh dill	1/2 cup	chopped fresh parsley
1/4 cup	chopped fresh basil	2 tbsp	light sour cream
1 tbsp	chili powder	1/2 cup	chopped fresh chives
1/2 tsp	salt		

Variation

Add 6 large grilled shrimp, chopped into pieces.

In a large soup pot or slow cooker, heat the oil; sauté the celery and onion for 1 minute. Add the garlic and sauté for another 2 minutes or until the onion is translucent; be careful not to burn the garlic. Add salsa, dill, basil, chili powder, salt, pepper, bay leaf and stock. Bring to a boil; reduce heat and simmer, stirring occasionally, 20 minutes. Stir in the beans and corn; cook another 2 minutes. Stir in the parsley. Remove the bay leaf. Serve garnished with a dollop of sour cream and the chives.

LowFatOption
Use 2 tbsp of vegetable stock instead of olive oil for sautéing.
274.6 cal.

A Mess of Vegetables

Spicy Vegetable Soup   52

Grilled Vegetable Soup with Fresh Herbs   53

Ken's French Onion Soup   54

Mixed Mushroom Soup with Fresh Herbs   55

Lentil Soup with Lemon and Parsley   56

Zesty Zucchini, Eggplant and Red Pepper Soup   57

Pumpkin Soup with Apple and Cinnamon   58

Beet Soup with Red Pepper and Roasted Garlic   59

Spicy Mixed Bell Pepper Soup with Red Wine   60

Artichoke and Asparagus Soup with White Wine   61

Celery and Cauliflower Soup with White Wine   62

Pesto Potato Soup with White Wine   63

Potato and Celery Soup with Herbs   64

Corn and Potato Soup   65

Peanut and Potato Soup   66

Mashed Potato Delight with Roasted Garlic and Cheese   67

Carrot, Potato and Leek Soup with Mint   68

Parsnip and Apple Soup with Maple Syrup   69

Spicy Vegetable Soup

It's the hot sauce and chili powder that add the "spicy" to this recipe.

Serves 8

<table>
<tr><td>1 tbsp</td><td>olive oil</td><td>1/2 cup</td><td>chopped cabbage</td></tr>
<tr><td>2</td><td>stalks celery, chopped</td><td>1/2 cup</td><td>chopped fresh basil</td></tr>
<tr><td>2</td><td>potatoes, diced</td><td>1/2 cup</td><td>chopped fresh parsley</td></tr>
<tr><td>2</td><td>carrots, chopped</td><td>1 tbsp</td><td>chili powder</td></tr>
<tr><td>1</td><td>small onion, chopped</td><td>1 tsp</td><td>hot pepper sauce</td></tr>
<tr><td>3</td><td>cloves garlic, chopped</td><td>1/2 tsp</td><td>salt</td></tr>
<tr><td>1</td><td>28-oz can tomatoes</td><td>1 tsp</td><td>black pepper</td></tr>
<tr><td>1</td><td>small zucchini, chopped</td><td>1</td><td>bay leaf</td></tr>
<tr><td>1/2 cup</td><td>chopped red bell pepper</td><td>6 cups</td><td>vegetable stock</td></tr>
</table>

Variation

Use any vegetables you like. This is a perfect soup for those leftover vegetables.

In a large soup pot or crock pot, heat the oil. Gently sauté the celery, potatoes, carrots and onion for 3 minutes. Add the garlic and sauté another 2 minutes. Stir in the tomatoes and their juice, zucchini, red pepper, cabbage, basil, parsley, chili powder, hot pepper sauce, salt, pepper, bay leaf and stock. Bring to a boil; reduce heat and simmer 15 to 20 minutes, until firm vegetables are tender. If the liquid evaporates, add water. Remove the bay leaf before serving.

LowFatOption

Use a non-stick pot and leave out the oil. Use low-fat vegetable stock.
67.3 cal.

Grilled Vegetable Soup with Fresh Herbs

I love grilled vegetables in a soup—they add a certain smoky something to the flavour. (If you haven't got an indoor grill, an outdoor one will do just fine.)

Serves 8

8	asparagus spears
2	large carrots, thickly sliced lengthwise
1	small zucchini, thickly sliced lengthwise
1	medium red onion, thickly sliced
1	large red bell pepper, cut into wide strips
1	large green bell pepper, cut into wide strips
1	large portobello mushroom
1	15-oz can stewed tomatoes
1/4 cup	chopped fresh basil OR 1/2 tsp dried
2 tbsp	balsamic vinegar OR lemon juice
1 1/2 tsp	chopped fresh oregano OR 1/4 tsp dried
1/2 tsp	black pepper
1/2 tsp	sea salt
1	bay leaf
8 cups	vegetable stock
1/2 cup	chopped fresh parsley

<aside>
LowFatOption
Use low-fat vegetable stock.
74.9 cal.
</aside>

Place the asparagus, carrots, zucchini, onion, red and green bell peppers and mushroom on a baking sheet. Spray both sides sparingly with cooking spray and grill for 5 minutes or until vegetables turn golden. Chop vegetables into bite-sized cubes. In a large soup pot, combine the tomatoes and their juice, basil, balsamic vinegar, oregano, black pepper, salt, bay leaf and stock. Bring to a boil and stir in grilled vegetables. Reduce heat and simmer another 8 minutes. Remove the bay leaf. Garnish with parsley and serve.

Ken's French Onion Soup

This is a soup to brag about: serve hot and start bragging. My French onion soup doesn't call for bread but it does call for gruyère cheese. (The secret to preventing the gruyère from sticking to the pot's bottom is to stir, stir and stir again.)

Serves 6

3 tbsp	unsalted butter
4	medium red onions, thinly sliced
2	cloves garlic, finely chopped
1/2 cup	dry red wine
1 tbsp	Dijon mustard
1 tbsp	balsamic vinegar
1 tsp	Worcestershire sauce
1/2 tsp	dried basil
1/2 tsp	dried thyme
1/2 tsp	salt
1/2 tsp	black pepper
1	bay leaf
7 cups	vegetable or beef stock
1 cup	grated gruyère cheese
	Grated Parmesan cheese

In a large soup pot, melt the butter. Add the onions and garlic; sauté for 5 minutes. Add the red wine and simmer for 3 to 4 minutes or until the mixture is reduced by half. Add the mustard, balsamic vinegar, Worcestershire sauce, basil, thyme, salt, pepper, bay leaf and stock. Simmer for 15 minutes. Remove the bay leaf. Add the gruyère cheese and simmer, stirring, for about 5 minutes. Garnish with Parmesan cheese and serve.

Mixed Mushroom Soup
with Fresh Herbs

The mixed mushrooms I chose for this recipe are exotic (portobellos, shiitakes) and homey (buttons), but please don't feel you have to use the same combination.

Serves 6

3 tbsp	olive oil
1	medium red onion, chopped
2	cloves garlic, chopped
1 cup	chopped button mushrooms
1 cup	chopped portobello mushrooms
1 cup	chopped shiitake mushrooms
1/4 cup	chopped fresh basil
2 tbsp	chopped fresh oregano
1 tbsp	chopped fresh thyme
2 tbsp	Dijon mustard
1 tbsp	Worcestershire sauce
1	bay leaf
8 cups	vegetable stock
1/4 cup	chopped fresh parsley

> ### Variation
> Add 1/2 cup red wine or 2 tbsp Port with the stock.

In a large soup pot, heat the oil. Sauté the onion, garlic and all the mushrooms until the mushrooms are releasing their liquid and have softened, about 6 to 8 minutes. Add the basil, oregano, thyme, mustard, Worcestershire sauce, bay leaf and stock. Bring to a boil; reduce heat and simmer 15 minutes. Remove the bay leaf and garnish with parsley before serving.

Lentil Soup with Lemon and Parsley

Hey! If you successfully sue a parsley farmer, can you garnish his wages?

Serves 6

1	medium red onion, chopped
	Juice of 3 lemons
1 tbsp	lemon zest
1 cup	finely chopped fresh parsley
1/2 tsp	dried basil
1/2 tsp	dried tarragon (optional)
1 tsp	black pepper
1/2 tsp	salt
1	bay leaf
6 cups	vegetable stock
1/2 cup	dry white wine (optional)
2 cups	cooked lentils
1 tsp	brown sugar

In a large soup pot, combine the onion, lemon juice, lemon zest, half of the parsley, basil, tarragon, pepper, salt, bay leaf, stock and wine. Bring to a boil; reduce heat and simmer 10 minutes. Add lentils and sugar. Simmer another 5 minutes. Remove bay leaf and garnish with the remaining parsley before serving.

Zesty Zucchini, Eggplant and Red Pepper Soup

The chili adds the zest and the zucchini-eggplant adds the heft. Enjoy!

Serves 6

2 tbsp	olive oil
1	small red onion, chopped
2	cloves garlic, finely chopped
1	small zucchini, peeled and cubed
1 cup	cubed eggplant
1	red bell pepper, chopped
1 tbsp	Dijon mustard
1 tbsp	Worcestershire sauce
1 tsp	chili powder
1/2 tsp	hot pepper flakes
1/2 tsp	dried basil
1/2 tsp	dried thyme
1/2 tsp	salt
1/2 tsp	black pepper
6 cups	vegetable stock
1 cup	table cream

LowFat**Option**

Replace olive oil with canola oil. Replace cream with skim milk or leave it out entirely.
242.3 cal.

In a large soup pot, heat the oil. Add the onion and garlic; sauté for 2 minutes or until the onion is translucent. Add the zucchini, eggplant and red pepper; sauté another 3 minutes. Add the mustard, Worcestershire sauce, chili powder, hot pepper flakes, basil, thyme, salt, black pepper and stock. Bring to a boil; reduce heat and simmer for 15 minutes. Using a hand blender, puree until smooth. Stir in the cream and simmer another 5 minutes or until heated through. Serve immediately.

Pumpkin Soup with Apple and Cinnamon

This is a smashing pumpkin soup! It's okay to use canned pumpkin, but I'd stick to using a good baking apple.

Serves 6

2 tbsp	unsalted butter
1	medium onion, chopped
2	apples, peeled, cored and cubed
2 cups	pureed cooked pumpkin
1/2 cup	apple juice
1/2 cup	applesauce
2 tbsp	brown sugar
1/2 tsp	cinnamon
1/2 tsp	dried thyme
1/2 tsp	salt
1/2 tsp	white pepper
1/4 tsp	ground nutmeg
1	bay leaf
6 cups	vegetable stock

In a large soup pot, melt the butter. Add the onion and apples; sauté for 3 to 4 minutes or until apples are tender. Stir in pumpkin, apple juice, applesauce, brown sugar, cinnamon, thyme, salt, pepper, nutmeg, bay leaf and stock. Bring to a boil; reduce heat and simmer for 15 minutes. Remove the bay leaf before serving.

Beet Soup with Red Pepper and Roasted Garlic

*Mama Kostick (Helen) prided herself on the borscht she so often
prepared for Papa Kostick (Ed) during their long and happy marriage.
This recipe is my tribute to the "beet" years of their lives.*

Serves 6

2 tbsp	olive oil
1	medium onion, chopped
2	red bell peppers, chopped
2 cups	canned beets, drained and diced
15	cloves roasted garlic (see page 23)
1/2 tsp	dried sage
1/2 tsp	dried basil
1/2 cup	red wine
1 tbsp	balsamic vinegar
1/2 tsp	salt
1/2 tsp	black pepper
1	bay leaf
7 cups	vegetable stock
1/2 cup	chopped fresh parsley

> **LowFatOption**
> Replace olive oil with
> canola oil. Use low-
> fat vegetable stock.
> 123.4 cal.

In a large soup pot, heat the oil. Add the onion and red peppers; sauté for 2 to 3
minutes or until the pepper is tender. Add the beets, roasted garlic, sage, basil and
wine. Simmer another 2 to 3 minutes, allowing the wine to reduce by half. Add
the balsamic vinegar, salt, black pepper, bay leaf and stock. Bring to a boil; reduce
heat and simmer 15 minutes. Remove the bay leaf and garnish with parsley before
serving.

Spicy Mixed Bell Pepper Soup with Red Wine

Sweet and hot peppers, joined by apple juice, red wine and balsamic vinegar, make this an incomparable soup du jour *any time of the year.*

Serves 6

3 tbsp	olive oil
1	medium onion, chopped
2	cloves garlic, chopped
1	red bell pepper, chopped
1	green bell pepper, chopped
1	yellow bell pepper, chopped
1 tbsp	finely chopped jalapeno pepper
1/2 cup	red wine
1 tbsp	balsamic vinegar
1/2 tsp	dried basil
1/2 tsp	sea salt
1/2 tsp	black pepper
5 cups	vegetable stock
1/2 cup	apple juice

Variation

Replace the apple juice with 1 cup applesauce for a very interesting texture as well as a delicious flavour.

In a large soup pot, heat the oil. Add onion and garlic; sauté 2 to 3 minutes or until the onion is translucent. Add the red, green and yellow peppers and the jalapeno; sauté another 5 minutes. Add the wine and simmer for 3 to 4 minutes or until the liquid is reduced by half. Add the balsamic vinegar, basil, salt, black pepper, stock and apple juice. Bring to a boil; reduce heat and simmer about 15 minutes. Using a hand blender, puree till smooth. Serve immediately.

Artichoke and Asparagus Soup
with White Wine

This is a triple whammy deluxe delight to serve when you're itching to impress guests.

Serves 6

3 tbsp	olive oil
1	medium onion, chopped
1	red bell pepper, chopped
2	cloves garlic, chopped
1 cup	chopped canned artichokes
10	asparagus spears, chopped
1/2 cup	dry white wine
1/2 cup	cooked white beans
1/2 cup	chopped fresh basil
1/2 tsp	sea salt
1/2 tsp	black pepper
1	bay leaf
6 cups	vegetable stock
1 cup	apple juice

Variation

Replace the apple juice with 1 cup table cream but add it just before serving; simmer it long enough to heat through.

In a large soup pot, heat the oil. Add onion, red pepper and garlic; sauté for 2 to 3 minutes or until the onion is translucent. Add the artichokes, asparagus and wine; simmer for 2 minutes. Add the beans, basil, salt, black pepper, bay leaf, stock and apple juice. Bring to a boil; reduce heat and simmer 15 minutes. Remove the bay leaf before serving.

Celery and Cauliflower Soup with White Wine

The white wine makes all the difference to this charming and subtly flavoured soup.

Serves 6

3 tbsp	olive oil
1	medium onion, chopped
2 cups	chopped cauliflower
1 1/2 cups	finely chopped celery
1/2 cup	dry white wine
1 tbsp	balsamic vinegar
1/2 tsp	dried basil
1/2 tsp	dried oregano
1/2 tsp	chili powder
1/2 tsp	sea salt
1/2 tsp	black pepper
1	bay leaf
6 cups	vegetable stock
1/2 cup	chopped fresh parsley

In a large soup pot, heat the oil. Add the onion, cauliflower and celery; sauté 4 to 5 minutes or until the cauliflower is tender. Add the wine and simmer 3 minutes. Add the balsamic vinegar, basil, oregano, chili powder, salt, pepper, bay leaf and stock. Bring to a boil; reduce heat and simmer 10 minutes. Remove the bay leaf. Garnish with parsley and serve immediately.

Pesto Potato Soup with White Wine

And now for something a little different …
(Wasn't Pesto the name of that other Marx brother?)

Serves 6

Soup

6 cups	vegetable stock
1 cup	dry white wine
1/2 tsp	dried thyme
1/2 tsp	salt
1/2 tsp	white pepper
2	medium potatoes, peeled and cubed
1	medium onion, chopped
2	cloves garlic, chopped
1	red bell pepper, chopped

Pesto sauce

1/2 cup	chopped fresh basil
1/2 cup	vegetable stock
1/4 cup	chopped fresh parsley
1/4 cup	grated Parmesan cheese
1 tbsp	pine nuts
1 tbsp	olive oil

LowFatOption

Use low-fat vegetable stock. Replace the olive oil with canola oil. Use low-fat Parmesan cheese. 114.9 cal.

In a large soup pot, combine stock, wine, thyme, salt and pepper; bring to a boil and reduce heat to a simmer. Add the potatoes, onion, garlic and red pepper. Simmer for 15 minutes. Meanwhile, combine the pesto ingredients in a blender and puree. Stir the pesto sauce into the soup and simmer another 5 minutes. Serve immediately.

Potato and Celery Soup
with Herbs

When three subtle flavours (potato, celery and bell pepper) mingle with basil, thyme, et al., you can bet the results will be delicious.

Serves 6

2 tbsp	olive oil		1/2 tsp	dried basil
2 cups	finely chopped celery with leaves		1/2 tsp	dried thyme
			1/2 tsp	salt
1	medium onion, chopped		1/2 tsp	black pepper
1/2	red bell pepper, chopped		6 cups	vegetable stock
2	cloves garlic, chopped		1/4 cup	grated Parmesan cheese
3	medium potatoes, peeled and cubed		1/4 cup	chopped fresh parsley

> ## Variation
> Replace celery with chopped fennel and add 1 oz ouzo or licorice liqueur.

In a large soup pot, heat the oil. Add the celery, onion, red pepper and garlic; sauté 2 minutes or until the onion is translucent. Add the potatoes, basil, thyme, salt, black pepper and stock. Simmer for 15 minutes or until the potatoes are cooked but not falling apart. Garnish with Parmesan and parsley and serve immediately.

> ## LowFatOption
> Replace olive oil with canola oil. Use low-fat vegetable stock. Use low-fat Parmesan cheese.
> 115.7 cal.

Corn and Potato Soup

This soup might serve 6 but it certainly rates a 10.

Serves 6

1	medium onion, chopped
2	cloves garlic, chopped
2 cups	mashed or diced cooked potatoes
2 cups	corn
1	red bell pepper, chopped
1 tbsp	Dijon mustard
1/2 tsp	dried basil
1/2 tsp	chili powder
1/2 tsp	sea salt
1/2 tsp	white pepper
6 cups	vegetable or chicken stock

> ### Variation
> Add any leftover vegetables to the soup.

In a large soup pot, combine the onion, garlic, potatoes, corn, red pepper, mustard, basil, chili powder, salt, white pepper and stock. Bring to a boil; reduce heat and simmer for 10 minutes. Using a hand blender, puree until smooth. Serve hot.

Peanut and Potato Soup

Actually, this recipe should be retitled "Peanuts,
Potatoes and More Peanuts Soup."

Serves 4 to 6

3	medium potatoes, cooked and cubed
1/2 cup	unsalted peanuts
2 tbsp	peanut butter
1/4 tsp	cinnamon (optional)
6 cups	vegetable stock
2 tbsp	olive oil
1	small onion, chopped
1/2 tsp	salt
1/2 tsp	black pepper
1/2 cup	table cream
1/4 cup	chopped fresh parsley

In a blender, combine potatoes, peanuts, peanut butter, cinnamon and 1 cup of the vegetable stock. Puree until smooth. In a large soup pot, heat the oil. Add onion; sauté 2 to 3 minutes or until translucent. Add remaining stock and bring to a boil; reduce heat and stir in the peanut mixture, salt and pepper. Simmer 10 minutes. Using a hand blender, puree the soup until smooth. Stir in cream, garnish with parsley and serve immediately.

LowFatOption

Replace olive oil with canola oil. Replace cream with 2 cooked potatoes, pureed. Use low-fat vegetable stock.
210.1 cal.

Mashed Potato Delight
with Roasted Garlic and Cheese

It's the mashed potatoes that makes this soup so delightful.

Serves 6

1	medium onion, chopped
10	cloves roasted garlic, chopped (see page 000)
1	red bell pepper, chopped
1 tbsp	Dijon mustard
1/2 tsp	dried basil
1/2 tsp	chili powder
1/2 tsp	sea salt
1/2 tsp	black pepper
6 cups	vegetable stock
3 cups	mashed potatoes
1/2 cup	shredded cheddar cheese
1/2 cup	table cream

> ### LowFatOption
> Replace the cheddar cheese with a cheddar-flavoured soy or rice cheese. Replace the cream with skim milk or soy milk.

In a large soup pot, combine the onion, roasted garlic, red pepper, mustard, basil, chili powder, salt, black pepper and stock. Bring to a boil; reduce heat and simmer 10 minutes. Add the mashed potatoes, cheese and cream. Simmer, stirring frequently, another 5 minutes. Serve immediately.

Carrot, Potato and Leek Soup with Mint

This combo of classic veggies gets a fresh kick with the addition of mint.

Serves 6

3 tbsp	olive oil
1	medium red onion, chopped
1 cup	grated carrot
1/2	leek, sliced
2	medium potatoes, peeled and cubed
1/4 cup	chopped fresh mint
1/4 cup	chopped fresh parsley
1 tbsp	sugar
1 tbsp	lemon juice
1/2 tsp	dried basil
1/2 tsp	sea salt
1/2 tsp	black pepper
6 cups	vegetable stock
1 cup	apple juice (optional)

Variation

Add 1/2 cup applesauce for a richer texture and flavour. Replace the sugar with 1 1/2 tsp honey.

In a large soup pot, heat the oil. Add the onion, carrot and leek; sauté for 3 to 4 minutes or until the carrot is tender. Add potatoes, mint, parsley, sugar, lemon juice, basil, salt, pepper, stock and apple juice, if using. Bring to a boil; reduce heat and simmer 15 minutes. Serve immediately.

Parsnip and Apple Soup with Maple Syrup

Growing up, I hated carrots, so you can imagine how I felt about the sun-deprived version known as parsnips. Well, that's all changed, and now I love parsnips: they're sweeter than carrots and nicely complement the apples in this soup.

Serves 6

3 tbsp	unsalted butter	1 tbsp	chopped fresh thyme OR	
4	parsnips, peeled and diced		1/4 tsp dried	
2	apples, cored and cubed	1 tbsp	maple syrup	
1	medium onion, chopped	1 tsp	Worcestershire sauce	
1/2 cup	dry white wine	1 tsp	balsamic vinegar (optional)	
6 cups	vegetable stock	1/2 tsp	cinnamon	
1 cup	apple juice	1/2 tsp	salt	
1/4 cup	chopped fresh basil OR	1/2 tsp	black pepper	
	1/2 tsp dried	1	bay leaf	

LowFatOption

Replace the butter with canola oil. Use low-fat vegetable stock. Use only 1 tsp maple syrup. 164.1 cal.

In a large soup pot, melt the butter. Add the parsnips, apples and onion; sauté 5 minutes or until parsnips are tender. Add the wine; simmer another 5 minutes or until the wine is reduced by half. Add stock, apple juice, basil, thyme, maple syrup, Worcestershire sauce, balsamic vinegar, cinnamon, salt, pepper and bay leaf. Bring to a boil; reduce heat and simmer for 15 minutes. Remove the bay leaf. Serve immediately.

Chill, Baby

Gazpacho   72

Way Down South Gazpacho   73

Chilled Borscht with Sour Cream   74

Cool Fennel Soup   75

Chilled Cucumber Mint Soup   76

Chilled Avocado and Pear Soup   77

Chilled Apple and Pear Soup   78

Chilled Apple Cinnamon Soup   79

Chilled Peach Soup with Parsley   80

Chilled Strawberry Mint Soup   81

Chilled Honeydew Melon Soup with Cinnamon   82

Chilled Pineapple and Coconut Soup   83

Gazpacho

The Spanish created this chilled meal in a bowl. It's perfect for those hot summer days in Sevilla, or Saskatoon, whatever your pleasure.

Serves 6

LowFatOption
Use a low-fat vegetable stock.
88.1 cal.

1	28-oz can stewed tomatoes, chopped
2	medium plum tomatoes, chopped
2	stalks celery, chopped
1	red bell pepper, chopped
1	green bell pepper, chopped
1	small cucumber, diced
1	small onion, chopped
1/2 cup	chopped fresh parsley
2 tbsp	chopped fresh basil
1 tbsp	chopped fresh dill
1 tbsp	chili powder
1/2 tsp	black pepper
1/2 tsp	salt
4 cups	vegetable stock
2 cups	tomato juice
2 tbsp	red wine vinegar or lemon juice

In a large bowl, stir together well the canned tomatoes and their juice, plum tomatoes, celery, red and green peppers, cucumber, onion, parsley, basil, dill, chili powder, black pepper, salt, stock, tomato juice and vinegar. Refrigerate for at least 1 hour before serving. Serve cold.

Way Down South Gazpacho

This is a Spanish classic with a creole accent! Enjoy.

Serves 6

4 cups	vegetable stock		1	green bell pepper, chopped
1	small zucchini, diced		1 tsp	finely chopped jalapeno
2	stalks celery, chopped			pepper (optional)
8	asparagus spears, chopped		1/2 cup	chopped fresh coriander
1	14-oz can stewed tomatoes		1/4 cup	chopped fresh parsley
1	small cucumber, diced			(plus additional for garnish)
1	onion, chopped		2 tbsp	chopped fresh basil
1	medium carrot, grated		2 cups	tomato juice
2	cloves garlic, chopped		2 tbsp	lemon juice
1	red bell pepper, chopped		2 tbsp	balsamic vinegar

In a large soup pot, bring 2 cups of the stock to a boil. Gently blanch the zucchini, celery and asparagus about 2 minutes. Remove the vegetables, and allow the vegetables and stock to cool. Return the blanched vegetables to the stock and add the stewed tomatoes and their juice, cucumber, onion, carrot, garlic, red and green peppers, jalapeno pepper, coriander, parsley, basil, tomato juice, lemon juice and balsamic vinegar. Mix well. If the soup is too thick, add more tomato juice, but keep in mind that this soup is like a fresh salad and should be quite chunky. Refrigerate at least 1 hour before serving. Serve cool, not ice cold, and garnish with fresh parsley.

Chilled Borscht with Sour Cream

"Borscht" is just an exotic (eastern European) name for beet soup; whatever you decide to call it, this recipe certainly "beets" most borscht.

Serves 6

1	14-oz can beets, drained and diced
2	stalks celery with leaves, chopped
1	small onion, chopped
1	clove garlic, finely chopped
5 cups	vegetable stock
1 cup	sour cream
1/2 cup	chopped fresh dill
1/2 tsp	dried basil
1/2 tsp	black pepper

In a food processor, combine beets, celery, onion, garlic, stock, sour cream, dill, basil and pepper; puree until nice and smooth. Chill for at least 1 hour before serving.

Low**Fat**Option
Replace sour cream with low-fat sour cream. Use low-fat vegetable stock. 73.2 cal.

Cool Fennel Soup

In case you're not an avid watcher of What's for Dinner? *I'll just reiterate:*
I love fennel! (It's my favourite ingredient.)

Serves 6

2 tbsp	olive oil
2 cups	finely chopped fennel
1	medium red onion, finely chopped
2	stalks celery, finely chopped
1	red bell pepper, finely chopped
1/2 cup	dry white wine
5 cups	vegetable stock
1 cup	apple juice
1/4 cup	chopped fresh mint
1/4 cup	chopped fresh basil
1/2 tsp	salt
1/2 tsp	white pepper
1/4 cup	chopped fresh parsley

In a large soup pot, heat the oil; sauté the fennel, onion, celery and red pepper for 5 minutes. Add the wine and simmer another 3 minutes. Add the stock, apple juice, mint, basil, salt and white pepper. Simmer 10 minutes. Refrigerate for at least 2 hours. Serve garnished with parsley.

Chilled Cucumber Mint Soup

Delicate and sublime in its flavours, this soup tastes great.

Serves 6

Variation

Replace the parsley with tarragon.

2	large cucumbers, peeled and chopped
1	small onion, chopped
1	clove garlic, chopped
2 cups	non-fat plain yogurt
1/2 cup	chopped fresh parsley
1/2 cup	chopped fresh mint
2 tbsp	lemon juice
1 tbsp	balsamic vinegar
1/2 tsp	black pepper
4 cups	vegetable stock
	Diced cucumber for garnish

In a blender or food processor, combine the cucumbers, onion, garlic, yogurt, parsley, half of the mint, lemon juice, balsamic vinegar, pepper and stock; puree until smooth. Refrigerate at least 1 hour before serving. Garnish with remaining mint and diced cucumber.

Chilled Avocado and Pear Soup

*The combination of avocado and pear makes for an
incredibly rich soup, in flavour and substance.*

Serves 6

4 cups	vegetable stock
2	pears, peeled, cored and chopped
2	shallots, chopped
4	ripe avocados, chopped
2 cups	pear juice
1/2 cup	sour cream
1/4 cup	finely chopped fresh basil
2 tbsp	dry sherry OR Port
1 tbsp	finely chopped fresh thyme
1 tsp	balsamic vinegar
1/2 tsp	salt
1/2 tsp	white pepper
1/4 cup	chopped fresh parsley

In a large soup pot, bring 1 cup of the stock to a boil. Add the pears and shallots;
simmer for 5 minutes. Remove the pot from the heat and add the avocados, pear
juice, sour cream, basil, sherry, thyme, balsamic vinegar, salt, pepper and remaining stock. Using a hand blender, puree till nice and smooth. If soup is too thick,
add some more pear juice or stock. Refrigerate for at least 2 hours. Serve garnished with parsley.

Chilled Apple and Pear Soup

*Although you could replace the pears with the apples or the apples
with the pears, the two wonderfully complement each other—
in the flavour department, that is.*

Serves 8

LowFatOption
Replace cream with
low-fat or non-fat
yogurt.
167.9 cal.

2	pears, peeled, cored and chopped
2	apples, peeled, cored and chopped
3 cups	pear nectar
3 cups	apple juice
1/2 cup	dry white wine
2 tbsp	frozen apple juice concentrate
1/2 tsp	cinnamon
1/4 tsp	ground nutmeg
1/2 cup	whipping cream
1/4 cup	chopped fresh parsley

In a large bowl, combine the pears, apples, pear nectar, apple juice, wine, apple
juice concentrate, cinnamon and nutmeg. In a food processor, puree the mixture
(in batches, if necessary). Stir the whipping cream into the soup and chill.
Garnish with parsley before serving.

Chilled Apple Cinnamon Soup

I hope they include this in the next "In Cider's Report."
Serve it on a hot day or for a hot date!

Serves 4

4	apples, peeled, cored and chopped
3 cups	apple juice
1 cup	vegetable stock (low sodium or low fat)
1/2 cup	lemon juice
1/2 cup	applesauce
1/2 tsp	cinnamon
1/2 cup	sour cream
1 tbsp	lemon juice

In a large soup pot, combine the apples, apple juice, stock, lemon juice, apple-sauce and cinnamon; bring to a boil and boil for 5 minutes. Puree in a blender or with a hand blender. Cool in the refrigerator. Whisk in the sour cream and lemon juice. Chill well before serving.

LowFatOption
Replace the sour cream with 1 cup non-fat yogurt (mix well) or use non-fat sour cream.
149.6 cal.

Chilled Peach Soup with Parsley

Without the peaches, this soup's the pits!

Serves 4

4	medium peaches, chopped
2 cups	orange juice
2 cups	peach nectar
1 cup	plain yogurt
1/4 cup	chopped fresh parsley
1 tbsp	lemon juice
1 tsp	brown sugar

In a large bowl, combine the peaches, orange juice, peach nectar, yogurt, parsley, lemon juice and sugar. In a food processor, puree the mixture (in batches, if necessary), or use a hand blender. Chill well before serving.

Low**FatOption**

Use non-fat or low-fat yogurt. Replace brown sugar with a calorie-reduced liquid sweetener.
229.6 cal.

Chilled Strawberry Mint Soup

This soup is a great starter with a meat or seafood
main course any time of the year.

Serves 6

3 1/2 cups	fresh strawberries, chopped
2 cups	plain yogurt
2 cups	cranberry juice
1/2 cup	dry red wine
1/2 cup	table cream
1/4 cup	chopped fresh mint

In a large mixing bowl combine 3 cups of the strawberries, yogurt, cranberry juice, wine, cream and mint. In a food processor, puree the mixture (in batches, if necessary). Chill about 1 hour before serving. Serve in individual bowls garnished with strawberry slices.

LowFatOption

Use non-fat yogurt. Replace the cream with skim milk. Use a light cranberry juice.
121.9 cal.

Chilled Honeydew Melon Soup with Cinnamon

This is a low-fat winner. Just try it!

Serves 6

1	large honeydew melon, diced
2 cups	unsweetened apple juice
2 cups	vegetable stock
1 cup	non-fat yogurt
1/4 cup	finely chopped fresh mint
2 tbsp	lemon juice
1/4 tsp	ground cinnamon OR 2 cinnamon sticks
2 tbsp	finely chopped fresh parsley

In a food processor or blender, combine the melon, apple juice, stock, yogurt, mint, lemon juice and ground cinnamon (if using). Puree until smooth. Add the cinnamon sticks (if using) and refrigerate for several hours to allow flavours to blend. Remove the cinnamon sticks before serving. Garnish with parsley.

Chilled Pineapple and Coconut Soup

This is a tropical delight, great before or after a meal.

Serves 6

4 cups	chopped pineapple
4 cups	pineapple juice
1 cup	plain yogurt
1 cup	apple juice
1 cup	unsweetened coconut milk
1/2 cup	unsweetened coconut flakes
1/2 tsp	cinnamon
1/4 tsp	ground nutmeg

In a large bowl, combine pineapple, pineapple juice, yogurt, apple juice, coconut milk, coconut flakes, cinnamon and nutmeg. In a food processor, puree the mixture (in batches, if necessary). Chill the soup at least 1 hour before serving. Garnish with a sprinkle of cinnamon.

LowFatOption
Use low-fat or non-fat yogurt. Use light coconut milk.
161.1 cal.

Lighten Up

Low-Fat Minestrone with Fresh Sage   86

Quick-and-Easy Vegetable Soup with Fresh Herbs and Red Wine   87

Cool Vegetable Soup with Herbs   88

Carrot and Ginger Mint Soup   89

Mushroom and Pasta Soup with Black Forest Ham   90

Simple Mushroom Soup with Potato and Sour Cream   91

Celery and Potato Soup with Feta and Rosemary   92

Potato and Cauliflower Soup with Coriander   93

Butternut Squash Soup with Curry and Apple   94

Spicy Tomato and Seafood Soup   95

Low-Fat Clam Chowder   96

Turkey Chowder   97

Low-Fat Chicken and Macaroni Soup with Salsa   98

Chicken and Rice Soup with Spinach and White Wine   99

Low-Fat Beef and Curry Soup with Yogurt   100

Hamburger and Chili Soup   101

Low-Fat Minestrone with Fresh Sage

Fresh sage adds a wonderful flavour to this not-so-traditional minestrone.

Serves 8

PER SERVING:

59 calories;

less than 1 g fat

(6% calories from fat);

3 g protein;

12 g carbohydrate;

0 mg cholesterol;

235 mg sodium

1	28-oz can stewed tomatoes, diced
1	medium onion, chopped
2	cloves garlic, chopped
2	stalks celery, chopped
1	small zucchini, chopped
1/2 cup	macaroni
1/2 cup	shredded carrot
1/4 cup	chopped fresh basil
2 tbsp	chopped fresh sage
1/2 tsp	sea salt
1/2 tsp	black pepper
1	bay leaf
7 cups	low-fat vegetable stock
1/4 cup	chopped fresh parsley
2 tbsp	grated non-fat Parmesan cheese

In a large soup pot, combine the tomatoes and their juice, onion, garlic, celery, zucchini, macaroni, carrot, basil, sage, salt, pepper, bay leaf and stock. Bring to a boil; reduce heat and simmer 10 to 12 minutes or until macaroni is cooked. Remove the bay leaf. Stir in the parsley and Parmesan. Serve immediately.

Variation
Add 1/2 cup red wine with the stock for added flavour.

86

Quick-and-Easy Vegetable Soup with Fresh Herbs and Red Wine

This winner has the great flavour of fresh herbs and red wine,
but only 57 calories per serving!

Serves 8

1	28-oz can stewed tomatoes, diced	1/2 tsp	black pepper
1	small onion, chopped	1	bay leaf
2	cloves garlic, chopped	6 cups	low-fat vegetable stock
1/2 cup	red wine	2	medium carrots, grated
1/4 cup	chopped fresh basil	1	small zucchini, chopped
1/4 cup	chopped fresh parsley	1	small red bell pepper, chopped
1 tbsp	chopped fresh rosemary	1/2 cup	frozen peas
1 tbsp	chopped fresh thyme	1/2 cup	frozen corn
1 tbsp	light soy sauce		

PER SERVING:

57 calories;

less than 1 g fat

(8% calories from fat);

2 g protein;

10 g carbohydrate;

0 mg cholesterol;

96 mg sodium

In a large soup pot, combine the stewed tomatoes and their juice, onion, garlic, wine, basil, parsley, rosemary, thyme, soy sauce, black pepper, bay leaf and stock. Bring to a boil; reduce heat and simmer 10 minutes. Add the carrots, zucchini, red pepper, peas and corn. Simmer another 5 minutes or until vegetables are cooked. Remove the bay leaf. Serve immediately.

Cool Vegetable Soup with Herbs

*Chilled and low fat, yet filling. Try this for dinner
on a long, hot summer's eve.*

Serves 8

PER SERVING:
22 calories;
less than 1 g fat
(9% calories from fat);
1 g protein;
4 g carbohydrate;
0 mg cholesterol;
207 mg sodium

1 cup	chopped broccoli
1 cup	chopped cauliflower
1/2 cup	chopped carrots
1/2 cup	chopped zucchini
1	medium onion, chopped
1 tsp	chili powder
1/2 tsp	dried basil
1/2 tsp	dried oregano
1/2 tsp	sea salt
1/2 tsp	black pepper
7 cups	low-fat vegetable stock
1/4 cup	chopped parsley

In a large soup pot, combine the broccoli, cauliflower, carrots, zucchini, onion, chili powder, basil, oregano, salt, pepper and stock. Bring to a boil; reduce heat and simmer 10 minutes. Using a hand blender, puree the soup until smooth. Let cool, then refrigerate for at least 2 hours. Garnish with parsley before serving.

Variation

Use any leftover vegetables, whether frozen or not.

Carrot and Ginger Mint Soup

"Zingy" is perhaps the best way to describe this taste sensation.

Serves 6

3 cups	grated carrot
1	medium onion, chopped
1/2 cup	white rice
1/4 cup	chopped fresh mint
1 tbsp	finely chopped fresh ginger
1/2 tsp	dried basil
1/2 tsp	chili powder
1/2 tsp	salt
1/2 tsp	black pepper
6 cups	low-fat vegetable stock
1 cup	apple juice
1/4 cup	chopped fresh parsley

PER SERVING:

141 calories;

1 g fat

(4% calories from fat);

4 g protein;

32 g carbohydrate;

0 mg cholesterol;

323 mg sodium

In a large soup pot, combine the carrots, onion, rice, mint, ginger, basil, chili powder, salt, pepper, stock and apple juice. Bring to a boil; reduce heat and simmer 15 minutes. Using a hand blender, blend until smooth. Garnish with parsley and serve immediately.

Variation

Replace the rice with 2 chopped potatoes to thicken. Replace mint with another 1/4 cup parsley.

Mushroom and Pasta Soup with Black Forest Ham

If you don't have black forest ham, any ham will do. As for the mushrooms?
Buttons are as good as anything else.

Serves 8

PER SERVING:
26 calories;
less than 1 g fat
(12% calories from fat);
2 g protein;
5 g carbohydrate;
0 mg cholesterol;
220 mg sodium

3 cups	chopped mushrooms
1	small onion, chopped
1	small red bell pepper, chopped
1/2 cup	bow tie pasta
1/4 cup	chopped fresh basil
1 tbsp	chopped fresh thyme
1 tbsp	Dijon mustard
1 tsp	balsamic vinegar
1/2 tsp	sea salt
1/2 tsp	black pepper
6 cups	low-fat vegetable stock
1/2 cup	chopped black forest ham
1/4 cup	chopped fresh parsley

In a large soup pot, combine the mushrooms, onion, red pepper, bow tie pasta, basil, thyme, mustard, balsamic vinegar, salt, black pepper and stock. Bring to a boil; reduce heat and simmer 10 minutes or until the pasta is cooked. Stir in the ham and parsley and heat through. Serve immediately.

Variation
Replace black forest ham with turkey.

Simple Mushroom Soup with Potato and Sour Cream

Unlike the "Complicated Mushroom Soup with Potato and Sour Cream," this soup can be tossed together in 20 minutes or less.

Serves 8

PER SERVING:
56 calories;
1 g fat
(8% calories from fat);
2 g protein;
12 g carbohydrate;
0 mg cholesterol;
246 mg sodium

3 cups	chopped button mushrooms
2	medium potatoes, peeled and cubed
1	medium onion, chopped
2 tbsp	Dijon mustard
1 tbsp	balsamic vinegar (optional)
1/2 tsp	dried basil
1/2 tsp	dried oregano
1/2 tsp	dried thyme
1/2 tsp	black pepper
1	bay leaf
6 cups	low-fat vegetable stock
1 cup	apple juice
1/2 cup	low-fat sour cream
1/2 cup	chopped fresh parsley

In a large soup pot, combine the mushrooms, potatoes, onion, mustard, balsamic vinegar, basil, oregano, thyme, pepper, bay leaf, stock and apple juice. Bring to a boil; reduce heat and simmer 15 minutes. Remove the bay leaf and using a hand blender puree till smooth. Add the sour cream and blend another minute. Stir in the parsley and serve immediately.

Celery and Potato Soup with Feta and Rosemary

This soup's a stand-out … everyone tells me so. The bonus, of course, is that it's low in fat too!

Serves 6

7 cups	low-fat vegetable stock
3 cups	chopped celery
1	medium onion, chopped
1/4 cup	dry white wine
2	medium potatoes, peeled and cubed
1 tbsp	Dijon mustard
2 tsp	chopped fresh rosemary
1/2 tsp	sea salt
1/2 tsp	black pepper
1	bay leaf
1/2 cup	crumbled light feta cheese
1/2 cup	chopped fresh parsley

In a large soup pot, bring 1/2 cup of the stock to a boil. Add the celery and onion; sauté gently for 4 minutes. Add the wine; sauté another 2 minutes. Add the potatoes, mustard, rosemary, salt, pepper, bay leaf and remaining stock. Bring to a boil; reduce heat and simmer 15 minutes or until potatoes are cooked. Remove the bay leaf. Stir in the feta cheese and parsley. Serve immediately.

Potato and Cauliflower Soup with Coriander

I'm sure you're thinking potatoes and low-fat don't go together, but one serving of this soup is only 34 calories!

Serves 8

3 cups	cauliflower florets
2	medium potatoes, peeled and cubed
1	medium onion, chopped
1	small red bell pepper, chopped
1/2 tsp	dried basil
1/2 tsp	dried oregano
1/2 tsp	black pepper
1	bay leaf
7 cups	low-fat vegetable stock
1/2 cup	chopped fresh coriander
1/2 cup	applesauce (optional)

PER SERVING:

34 calories;

less than 1 g fat

(4% calories from fat);

1 g protein;

7 g carbohydrate;

0 mg cholesterol;

82 mg sodium

In a large soup pot, combine the cauliflower, potatoes, onion, red pepper, basil, oregano, black pepper, bay leaf and stock. Bring to a boil; reduce heat and simmer 10 minutes. Add the coriander and applesauce; simmer another 5 minutes. Remove the bay leaf. Serve immediately.

Butternut Squash Soup with Curry and Apple

Never mind the calories: there's less than 1 gram of fat in one serving of this hearty soup.

Serves 8

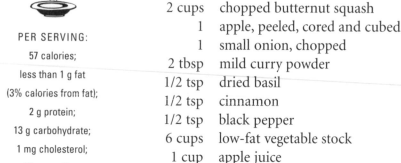

PER SERVING:

57 calories;

less than 1 g fat

(3% calories from fat);

2 g protein;

13 g carbohydrate;

1 mg cholesterol;

93 mg sodium

2 cups	chopped butternut squash
1	apple, peeled, cored and cubed
1	small onion, chopped
2 tbsp	mild curry powder
1/2 tsp	dried basil
1/2 tsp	cinnamon
1/2 tsp	black pepper
6 cups	low-fat vegetable stock
1 cup	apple juice
1 cup	non-fat yogurt

In a large soup pot, combine the squash, apple, onion, curry powder, basil, cinnamon, black pepper, stock and apple juice. Bring to a boil; reduce heat and simmer 15 minutes or until squash is tender. Using a hand blender, puree the soup till smooth. Add the non-fat yogurt and continue to blend till creamy. Serve immediately.

Spicy Tomato and Seafood Soup

If you can't stand the heat, don't even think of serving this one;
on a scale of 1 to 5, this is an eye-popping 6!

Serves 8

1	28-oz can stewed tomatoes
1	medium onion, chopped
1/2 cup	chopped fresh basil
1/2 cup	chopped fresh parsley
1/2 tsp	hot pepper flakes
1/2 tsp	black pepper
1	bay leaf
5 cups	low-fat fish or vegetable stock
1 cup	tomato juice
1/2 cup	red wine
1 cup	peeled baby shrimp
1 cup	small scallops
1 cup	squid chopped into small rings
4	medium tomatoes, chopped

PER SERVING:

80 calories;

1 g fat

(9% calories from fat);

7 g protein;

11 g carbohydrate;

10 mg cholesterol;

251 mg sodium

In a large soup pot, combine stewed tomatoes and their juice, onion, basil, parsley, hot pepper flakes, black pepper, bay leaf, stock, tomato juice and wine. Bring to a boil; reduce heat and simmer 10 minutes. Add shrimp, scallops, squid and chopped tomatoes. Simmer another 5 minutes. Remove the bay leaf and serve immediately.

Low-Fat Clam Chowder

*What can I say except: you'll be as happy as a clam
once you try this tasty low-fat chowder.*

Serves 8

PER SERVING:

73 calories;

1 g fat

(7% calories from fat);

6 g protein;

12 g carbohydrate;

8 mg cholesterol;

200 mg sodium

2	medium potatoes, peeled and cubed
2	stalks celery, chopped
1	carrot, grated
1	small red bell pepper, chopped
1	medium red onion, chopped
1	tomato, chopped or diced
1 cup	canned clams
1 tbsp	Dijon mustard
1/2 tsp	dried basil
1/2 tsp	chili powder
1/2 tsp	sea salt
1/2 tsp	black pepper
2 cups	low-fat vegetable stock
2 cups	low-fat fish stock
2 cups	skim milk
1/4 cup	chopped fresh chives

Variation
Replace clams with
1 cup shrimp.

In a large soup pot, combine potatoes, celery, carrot, red pepper, onion, tomato, clams, mustard, basil, chili powder, salt, black pepper, vegetable stock and fish stock. Bring to a boil; reduce heat and simmer 10 minutes. Stir in skim milk and chives. Serve immediately.

Turkey Chowder

*This is the perfect solution for all those turkey leftovers—
and for chicken leftovers, too.*

Serves 8

1	medium onion, chopped	1 1/2 tsp	chili powder
1	medium potato, peeled and cubed	1 tsp	Worcestershire sauce
2 cups	cubed cooked turkey	1/2 tsp	dried sage
1/2 cup	grated carrot	1/2 tsp	dried rosemary
1/2 cup	frozen corn	1/2 tsp	sea salt
1/2 cup	frozen peas	1/2 tsp	white pepper
1 tbsp	horseradish	4 cups	low-fat chicken stock
		2 cups	skim milk

PER SERVING:

99 calories;

2 g fat

(14% calories from fat);

11 g protein;

11 g carbohydrate;

19 mg cholesterol;

264 mg sodium

In a large soup pot, combine the onion, potato, turkey, carrot, corn, peas, horseradish, chili powder, Worcestershire sauce, sage, rosemary, salt, pepper and stock. Bring to a boil; reduce heat and simmer 10 minutes or until the potato is cooked. Stir in the skim milk and simmer another 2 minutes. Serve immediately.

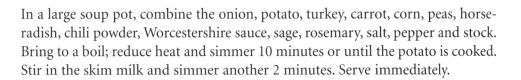

Variation

Add 1/2 cup white wine with the stock. Replace turkey with chicken.

Low-Fat Chicken and Macaroni Soup with Salsa

You really don't have to feel like you're depriving yourself when serving low-fat soup. This one proves my point.

Serves 8

PER SERVING:
131 calories;
5 g fat
(32% calories from fat);
13 g protein;
10 g carbohydrate;
33 mg cholesterol;
268 mg sodium

1	28-oz can stewed tomatoes, diced	1/2 tsp	chili powder
2 cups	cubed cooked chicken	1/2 tsp	dried basil
1 cup	salsa	1/2 tsp	dried sage
1/2 cup	macaroni	1/2 tsp	sea salt
2	stalks celery, chopped	1/2 tsp	black pepper
1	medium onion, chopped	1	bay leaf
2	cloves garlic, chopped	6 cups	low-fat chicken stock
		1/2 cup	chopped fresh parsley

In a large soup pot, combine the stewed tomatoes and their juice, chicken, salsa, macaroni, celery, onion, garlic, chili powder, basil, sage, salt, pepper, bay leaf and stock. Bring to a boil; reduce heat and simmer for 10 to 12 minutes or until the macaroni is cooked. Remove the bay leaf. Stir in the parsley and serve immediately.

Variation

Replace chicken with turkey. Use a combination of low-fat chicken stock and low-fat vegetable stock.

Chicken and Rice Soup with Spinach and White Wine

This is simply divine, simmered with white wine.

Serves 8

3 tbsp	olive oil
2	stalks celery, chopped
1	small red bell pepper, chopped
1	medium red onion, chopped
2	cloves garlic, chopped
1/2 cup	dry white wine
3 cups	finely chopped spinach
2 cups	cubed cooked chicken
1/2 cup	rice
1/2 tsp	dried basil
1/2 tsp	dried oregano
1/2 tsp	dried rosemary
1/2 tsp	sea salt
1/2 tsp	black pepper
1	bay leaf
7 cups	low-fat chicken stock

PER SERVING:

188 calories;

8 g fat

(42% calories from fat);

12 g protein;

13 g carbohydrate;

32 mg cholesterol;

171 mg sodium

In a large soup pot, heat the oil. Add the celery, red pepper, onion and garlic; sauté 2 minutes or until the onion is translucent. Add the wine; simmer until the mixture is reduced by half. Add the spinach, chicken, rice, basil, oregano, rosemary, salt, black pepper, bay leaf and stock. Bring to a boil; reduce heat and simmer for 15 minutes. Remove the bay leaf and serve immediately.

Variation

Replace rice with a small pasta.

Low-Fat Beef and Curry Soup with Yogurt

Whenever I make this soup, I freeze a portion of it, ready to throw into a sauce and serve over hot rice or pasta.

Serves 6

PER SERVING:

191 calories;

12 g fat

(55% calories from fat);

16 g protein;

5 g carbohydrate;

45 mg cholesterol;

326 mg sodium

1 tbsp	olive oil
1 lb	round steak, cut into bite-sized pieces
1	medium onion, chopped
2	cloves garlic, chopped
1	red bell pepper, chopped
1	carrot, grated
1 tbsp	mild curry powder

1/2 tsp	dried basil
1/2 tsp	salt
1/2 tsp	black pepper
1	bay leaf
6 cups	low-fat beef stock
1/2 cup	non-fat yogurt
1/4 cup	chopped fresh coriander

In a large soup pot, heat the oil. Add beef and sauté for 3 minutes. Add the onion, garlic, red pepper and carrot; sauté for 2 minutes. Add the curry powder, basil, salt, black pepper, bay leaf and stock. Bring to a boil; reduce heat and simmer for 10 minutes. Remove the bay leaf. Serve immediately garnished with yogurt and coriander.

Variation

Replace beef with very lean pork.

Hamburger and Chili Soup

This is the best one-pot meal; serve for dinner or lunch.

Serves 8

1/2 lb	lean ground beef
1	28-oz can stewed tomatoes, diced
2	stalks celery, chopped
1	red bell pepper, chopped
1	medium onion, chopped
1/2	carrot, shredded
2	cloves garlic, chopped
1/2 cup	cooked red beans
1 tbsp	chili powder
1/2 tsp	dried basil
1/2 tsp	salt
1/2 tsp	black pepper
1/4 tsp	hot pepper flakes
1	bay leaf
7 cups	low-fat vegetable stock
1/2 cup	chopped fresh coriander

PER SERVING:

128 calories;

6 g fat

(43% calories from fat);

8 g protein;

10 g carbohydrate;

21 mg cholesterol;

244 mg sodium

In a large soup pot, sauté the ground beef for 5 minutes or until no longer pink. Remove and drain on paper towel. In the same pot, combine the stewed tomatoes and their juice, celery, red pepper, onion, carrot, garlic, beans, chili powder, basil, salt, black pepper, hot pepper flakes, bay leaf and stock. Bring to a boil; reduce heat and simmer 10 minutes. Remove the bay leaf. Garnish with coriander and serve immediately.

Variation

Replace the lean ground beef with lean ground turkey.

Soup for the Sole

Sole and Red Snapper Soup with White Wine and Apple   104

Mediterranean Fish Chowder with Red Wine and Herbs   105

Fish Soup Italian-Style   106

Fish Soup with Pineapple and Coconut   107

Swordfish Soup with Coconut Milk and Rum   108

Swordfish Soup with Parsley and Lime   109

Quick Fish Chowder with Herbs   110

Salmon Chowder   111

Creole Conch Chowder   112

Traditional No-Cream Clam Soup   113

Creamy Clam Chowder   114

Tangy Tomato Clam Chowder   115

Mussel Tomato Soup with Basil   116

Mussel Soup with Lemon and Tarragon   117

Mussel Soup with Garlic and Coriander   118

Grilled Shrimp and Vegetable Chili Soup   119

Baby Shrimp Tomato Soup   120

Scallop Soup with Red Wine and Rosemary   121

Squid Soup with Roasted Garlic and Sage   122

Sole and Red Snapper Soup with White Wine and Apple

There's no doubt about it: this soup's good for the sole!

Serves 6

2	apples, peeled, cored and cubed
1	medium potato, peeled and cubed
1	stalk celery, chopped
1	large carrot, shredded
1	small onion, chopped
6 cups	vegetable stock
1 cup	apple juice or cider
1/2 cup	dry white wine
2 tbsp	lemon juice
1 tbsp	sugar
1/2 tsp	dried basil
1/2 tsp	dried thyme
1/2 tsp	salt
1/2 tsp	black pepper
1/4 tsp	cinnamon
3 cups	cubed assorted fish (sole, red snapper, swordfish, tuna and/or cod)
1/2 cup	chopped fresh parsley

In a large soup pot, combine the apples, potato, celery, carrot, onion, stock, apple juice, wine, lemon juice, sugar, basil, thyme, salt, pepper and cinnamon. Bring to a boil; reduce heat and simmer 15 minutes. Add the assorted fish; simmer for another 10 minutes. Stir in the parsley and serve immediately.

Mediterranean Fish Chowder with Red Wine and Herbs

*What makes this "Mediterranean" is, of course, the red peppers,
the red wine and the tomatoes (and the wonderful seafood).*

Serves 6 to 8

8 cups	fish or vegetable stock	1/2 tsp	dried oregano	
1	medium red onion, chopped	1/2 tsp	dried sage	
2	cloves garlic, minced	1/2 tsp	black pepper	
2	stalks celery, chopped	1	bay leaf	
2	carrots, chopped	1/2 cup	red wine	
1	red bell pepper, chopped	1 cup	canned clams, rinsed	
1	19-oz can stewed tomatoes, chopped	1	small swordfish steak, cubed (about 1 cup)	
1/2 tsp	dried basil	1 cup	medium shrimp, peeled	

LowFatOption

Use low-fat fish or
vegetable stock.
124.8 cal.

In a large soup pot, heat 2 tbsp of the stock; sauté the onion and garlic for 3 minutes (be careful not to burn the garlic). Add the celery, carrots and red pepper; gently sauté another 3 minutes. Add tomatoes and their juice, basil, oregano, sage, black pepper, bay leaf, red wine and remaining stock. Bring to a boil; reduce heat and simmer 15 minutes, stirring occasionally. Stir in clams, swordfish and shrimp. Simmer 5 to 7 minutes or until seafood is cooked. Remove bay leaf before serving.

Variation
Use other seafood such as squid, mussels and scallops.

Fish Soup Italian-Style

This is a meal in itself, and only 478 calories per serving.

Serves 6

1	28-oz can stewed tomatoes, diced
2	medium carrots, grated
2	stalks celery, chopped
1	red bell pepper, chopped
1	medium onion, chopped
2	cloves garlic, chopped
1/2 cup	chopped fresh basil
2 tbsp	chopped fresh rosemary
1 tbsp	chopped fresh thyme
1/2 tsp	sea salt
1/2 tsp	black pepper
7 cups	fish stock
1 cup	red wine
1/2 cup	cooked red beans
1/2 cup	cooked white beans
1	red snapper fillet, chopped
1 lb	squid, cut into pieces
1 lb	mussels, cleaned
1 cup	canned clams, rinsed
1/2 cup	chopped fresh parsley

In a large soup pot, combine stewed tomatoes and their juice, carrots, celery, red pepper, onion, garlic, basil, rosemary, thyme, salt, black pepper, stock and wine. Bring to a boil; reduce heat and simmer for 15 minutes. Add the red and white beans, snapper, squid, mussels and clams. Cover and simmer 4 to 5 minutes or until the mussels have opened. (Discard any mussels that do not open.) Garnish with parsley and serve.

Fish Soup with Pineapple and Coconut

Don't be put off by the pineapple: this is one of the most delicious soups on anyone's menu.

Serves 6

2 tbsp	olive oil
2	stalks celery, chopped
1	red bell pepper, chopped
1	medium red onion, chopped
2	cloves garlic, chopped
4 cups	fish stock
1 cup	pineapple juice
1 cup	sweetened coconut milk
1 tbsp	balsamic vinegar
1/2 tsp	dried basil
1/2 tsp	sea salt
1/2 tsp	white pepper
1 cup	finely chopped pineapple
1	large sole fillet, cut into bite-sized pieces
1	large red snapper fillet, cut into bite-sized pieces
1/4 cup	chopped fresh parsley

In a large soup pot, heat the oil. Sauté the celery, red pepper, onion and garlic for 2 minutes or until onion is translucent. Add the stock, pineapple juice, coconut milk, balsamic vinegar, basil, salt and white pepper. Simmer for 10 minutes. Add the pineapple, sole and red snapper. Simmer another 5 minutes. Gently stir in the parsley and serve.

Swordfish Soup with Coconut Milk and Rum

Rum and coconut make this a double-edged swordfish soup!

Serves 6

2 tbsp	olive oil
2	stalks celery, chopped
1	small red bell pepper, chopped
1	medium onion, chopped
2	cloves garlic, chopped
1 tbsp	grated fresh ginger
1/4 cup	dark rum
5 cups	fish stock
1 cup	sweetened coconut milk
1 tbsp	lemon juice
1/2 tsp	dried basil
1/2 tsp	dried tarragon (optional)
1/2 tsp	salt
1/2 tsp	white pepper
1	swordfish steak, chopped (about 2 cups)
1/4 cup	chopped fresh coriander
1/4 cup	chopped fresh parsley
1/4 cup	chopped green onion

In a large soup pot, heat the olive oil. Sauté the celery, red pepper, onion, garlic and ginger 3 minutes or until onion is translucent. Add the rum; allow the liquid to reduce for 3 to 4 minutes. Add the stock, coconut milk, lemon juice, basil, tarragon, if using, salt and white pepper. Reduce the heat and simmer 10 minutes. Add the swordfish and simmer another 5 minutes or until the swordfish is cooked. Stir in the coriander, parsley and green onion. Serve immediately.

Swordfish Soup with Parsley and Lime

The meat of the swordfish is lean, sweet and very firm,
which makes it a perfect addition to any soup.

Serves 4 to 6

2 tbsp	olive oil
1	medium onion, chopped
2	cloves garlic, chopped
1/2 cup	finely chopped celery
1/2 cup	shredded red bell pepper
1/2 cup	shredded green bell pepper
1/4 cup	grated carrot
3/4 cup	finely chopped fresh parsley
6 cups	fish stock
1 tbsp	balsamic vinegar
	Juice of 2 limes
1 tsp	lime zest
1 tsp	sugar
1/2 tsp	dried basil
1/2 tsp	salt
1/2 tsp	black pepper
1	swordfish steak, cut into bite-sized pieces

LowFatOption
Replace olive oil with canola oil. Use low-fat vegetable stock. 110.2 cal.

Variation
Replace swordfish with tuna steak.

In a large soup pot, heat the oil. Add the onion and garlic; sauté for 2 minutes or until the onion is translucent. Add the celery, red pepper, green pepper, carrot, 1/4 cup of the parsley, stock, balsamic vinegar, lime juice, lime zest, sugar, basil, salt and black pepper. Bring to a boil; reduce heat and simmer for 5 minutes. Add the swordfish; simmer another 5 to 6 minutes, being careful not to overcook the swordfish. Stir in the remaining parsley and serve immediately.

Quick Fish Chowder with Herbs

Although this fish chowder does call for fresh shrimp,
you can use the "already cooked" variety.

Serves 8

2 tbsp	olive oil
1	medium red onion, chopped
2	cloves garlic, minced
2	stalks celery, chopped
2	carrots, chopped
2	potatoes, cubed
1	red bell pepper, chopped
1 cup	chopped fennel (optional)
1	19-oz can stewed tomatoes, chopped
8 cups	fish or vegetable stock
1/2 tsp	dried basil
1/2 tsp	dried sage
1/2 tsp	dried thyme
1/2 tsp	black pepper
1 cup	canned clams, rinsed
1	small tuna steak, cubed (about 1 cup) OR 1 cup drained canned tuna
1 cup	medium shrimp, peeled and deveined
1/2 cup	chopped fresh parsley

In a large soup pot, heat the oil. Sauté the onion and garlic for 2 minutes, being careful not to burn the garlic. Add the celery, carrots, potatoes, red pepper and fennel; gently sauté for another 3 minutes. Add tomatoes and their juice, stock, basil, sage, thyme and black pepper. Bring to a boil; reduce heat and simmer 15 minutes, stirring occasionally. Stir in clams, tuna and shrimp. Simmer until seafood is cooked, about 5 minutes. Stir in parsley and serve.

Salmon Chowder

Salmon chowder is a variation on the more common seafood chowders.
It's delicious and very healthy.

Serves 6

2 tbsp	olive oil
4	shallots, chopped
2	stalks celery, chopped
1	leek, chopped
1	red bell pepper, chopped
2	medium potatoes, peeled and cubed
6 cups	fish or vegetable stock
1/2 cup	dry white wine
2	salmon steaks, boned and cubed
1	carrot, grated
1 tbsp	Dijon mustard
1/2 tsp	dried basil
1/2 tsp	dried sage
1/2 tsp	salt
1/2 tsp	black pepper
1	bay leaf
1/4 cup	chopped fresh dill

> **LowFatOption**
> Replace olive oil with
> 1/2 cup low-fat veg-
> etable stock to sauté.
> Use low-fat fish or
> vegetable stock.
> 160.2 cal.

In a large soup pot, heat the oil. Add shallots, celery, leek and red pepper; sauté 3 minutes or until shallots are translucent. Add potatoes; sauté another minute. Add the stock, wine, salmon, carrot, mustard, basil, sage, salt, black pepper and bay leaf. Bring to a boil; reduce heat and simmer for 15 minutes. Remove bay leaf and garnish with fresh dill before serving.

Creole Conch Chowder

This Caribbean-inspired chowder is hot, hot, hot!

Serves 4

2 tbsp	olive oil
4 cups	finely chopped skinless conch
1 tbsp	dried basil
1 tsp	dried oregano
1 tsp	cracked black pepper
1/2 tsp	finely chopped jalapeno pepper
1/2 tsp	salt
1	bay leaf
2	stalks celery, chopped
2	medium carrots, coarsely chopped
1	large potato, cubed
1	red bell pepper, chopped
1	medium onion, chopped
8 cups	fish stock OR water
1 cup	table cream

In a large soup pot, heat the oil. Add the conch, basil, oregano, black pepper, jalapeno pepper, salt and bay leaf. Cook for 5 minutes, stirring often. Add the celery, carrots, potato, red pepper and onion; cook for another 5 minutes. Add the fish stock; bring to a boil, reduce the heat and simmer for 20 minutes. Stir in the cream and simmer for another 5 minutes. Remove the bay leaf before serving.

Variation

Replace conch with 4 cups chopped squid.

Traditional No-Cream Clam Soup

For a delicious, no-guilt experience, try my low-fat,
no-cream clam soup.

Serves 6 to 8

2 tbsp	olive oil
2	stalks celery, chopped
1	green bell pepper, chopped
1	medium onion, chopped
2	cloves garlic, chopped
2	medium potatoes, cubed
2	plum tomatoes, chopped
1	medium carrot, shredded
1/2 tsp	dried basil
1/2 tsp	dried thyme
1/2 tsp	chili powder
1/2 tsp	salt
1/2 tsp	black pepper
7 cups	fish stock
1 cup	clam juice (optional) OR apple juice
1/2 cup	dry white wine
1 lb	whitefish (cod, halibut or sole), cubed
2 cups	canned clams, rinsed

LowFatOption

Use low-fat vegetable stock. Replace olive oil with 1/4 cup vegetable stock and sauté gently.
177.0 cal.

In a large soup pot, heat the oil. Add the celery, green pepper, onion and garlic; sauté for 3 minutes or until onion is translucent and pepper is tender. Add the potatoes, tomatoes, carrot, basil, thyme, chili powder, salt, black pepper, stock, clam juice, wine and whitefish; simmer for 10 minutes. Add the clams and simmer another 5 minutes. Serve immediately.

Creamy Clam Chowder

This creamy chowder is the best way to enjoy clams.

Serves 6

3 tbsp	unsalted butter
1/2 cup	grated carrot
2	stalks celery, chopped
1	red bell pepper, chopped
1	medium onion, chopped
2	cloves garlic, chopped
2	medium potatoes, peeled and cubed
1 1/2 cups	canned clams, rinsed
1/2 cup	dry white wine
1 tsp	chili powder
1/2 tsp	dried basil
1/2 tsp	dried thyme
1/2 tsp	sea salt
1/2 tsp	white pepper
8 cups	fish stock
1/2 cup	table cream
1/2 cup	whipping cream
1/2 cup	shredded cheddar cheese
1/4 cup	chopped fresh parsley

In a large soup pot, melt the butter. Add the carrot, celery, red pepper, onion and garlic; sauté for 2 minutes or until the onion is translucent. Add the potatoes, clams, wine, chili powder, basil, thyme, salt and white pepper; simmer 4 minutes. Add the fish stock; simmer 10 minutes. Add the table cream, whipping cream and cheese. Heat for another 5 minutes, stirring. Garnish with parsley and serve immediately.

Tangy Tomato Clam Chowder

Cocktail sauce, red wine, basil and thyme
add oomph to this chunky chowder.

Serves 8

2 tbsp	olive oil		1/2 tsp	salt
1	medium onion, chopped		1/2 tsp	dried basil
2	cloves garlic, chopped		1/2 tsp	dried thyme
1/2	green bell pepper, chopped		1	bay leaf
1	28-oz can stewed tomatoes		6 cups	fish stock
2	potatoes, peeled and cubed		1/2 cup	clam juice (optional)
1/2 cup	shrimp or seafood		1/2 cup	red wine
	cocktail sauce		1 cup	canned clams, rinsed
2 tbsp	Worcestershire sauce		1/4 cup	chopped fresh parsley
1 tsp	black pepper			

> **Variation**
>
> Replace clams with baby shrimp.

In a large soup pot, heat the oil. Add onion, garlic and green pepper; sauté for 3 minutes or until onion is translucent and pepper is tender. Add the stewed tomatoes and their juice, potatoes, seafood sauce, Worcestershire sauce, black pepper, salt, basil, thyme, bay leaf, stock, clam juice and wine. Simmer for 15 minutes or until potatoes are tender. Add the clams and simmer another 5 minutes. Remove the bay leaf. Garnish with parsley before serving.

LowFatOption
Replace olive oil with canola oil. Replace fish stock with low-fat fish or vegetable stock.
193.6 cal.

Mussel Tomato Soup with Basil

When buying mussels in the shell, make sure none are open.

Serves 4

1	28-oz can stewed tomatoes
2	tomatoes, chopped
1	red bell pepper, thinly sliced
1	medium onion, thinly sliced
2	cloves garlic, chopped
1/2 cup	chopped fresh basil
1/2 tsp	dried thyme
1/2 tsp	sugar
1/2 tsp	salt
1/2 tsp	black pepper
4 cups	fish stock
1/2 cup	red wine
1 tbsp	lemon juice
1 1/2 lb	mussels, cleaned
1/2 cup	finely chopped fresh parsley

LowFatOption
Use low-fat fish stock.
259.8 cal.

In a large soup pot, combine the stewed tomatoes and their juice, chopped tomatoes, red pepper, onion, garlic, basil, thyme, sugar, salt, black pepper, stock, wine and lemon juice. Bring to a boil; reduce heat and simmer for 10 minutes. Add the mussels and simmer, covered, 4 minutes or until the mussels open. (Discard any mussels that do not open.) Serve soup immediately, sprinkled with parsley.

Mussel Soup with Lemon and Tarragon

This mussel soup is the best version I've ever tasted.

Serves 6

3 tbsp	unsalted butter
2	stalks celery, julienned
1	red bell pepper, cut into strips
1	medium red onion, sliced
2	cloves garlic, chopped
1/2 cup	dry white wine
1/2 cup	chopped fresh tarragon
	Juice of 2 lemons
2 tbsp	lemon zest
1 tbsp	sugar
1/2 tsp	dried basil
1/2 tsp	salt
1/2 tsp	white pepper
6 cups	vegetable stock
1/2 cup	table cream
2 lb	mussels, cleaned

LowFatOption

Replace butter with canola oil. Use low-fat vegetable stock. Use skim milk instead of cream or leave it out completely. 252.1 cal.

In a large soup pot, melt the butter. Sauté the celery, red pepper, onion and garlic for 3 minutes. Add the wine and simmer another 3 minutes or until the wine has reduced slightly. Add half of the tarragon, the lemon juice, lemon zest, sugar, basil, salt, white pepper and stock. Bring to a boil; reduce heat and simmer 10 minutes. Stir in the cream and add the mussels. Cover and simmer another 5 minutes or until mussels open. (Discard any mussels that do not open.) Add remaining tarragon and serve immediately.

Mussel Soup with Garlic and Coriander

Make sure you have sticks of French bread when serving this;
you'll want to sop up the delicious broth!

Serves 6

1	28-oz can stewed tomatoes, diced
1	medium red onion, sliced
4	cloves garlic, chopped
1 tbsp	Dijon mustard
1 tsp	finely chopped fresh ginger
1/2 tsp	dried basil
1/2 tsp	dried sage
1/2 tsp	sea salt
1/2 tsp	black pepper
1	bay leaf
5 cups	fish stock
1/4 cup	red wine
1 1/2 lb	mussels, cleaned
1/2 cup	chopped fresh coriander
1/2 cup	chopped fresh parsley

In a large soup pot, combine the stewed tomatoes and their juice, onion, garlic, mustard, ginger, basil, sage, salt, black pepper, bay leaf, stock and wine. Bring to a boil; reduce heat and simmer for 10 minutes. Add the mussels; raise the heat and cover pot. Cook 4 minutes or until mussels open. (Discard any mussels that do not open.) Remove the bay leaf. Gently stir in coriander and parsley and serve immediately.

Grilled Shrimp and Vegetable Chili Soup

I always grill my shrimp on an indoor grill (it's fast and easy this way);
if you don't have an indoor grill, try the backyard barbecue or the oven.

Serves 8

2	carrots, thickly sliced lengthwise	1	28-oz can stewed tomatoes, diced
2	zucchini, thickly sliced lengthwise	1/2 cup	chopped fresh basil
2	stalks celery, cut into large pieces	2 tbsp	sugar
1	large onion, cut into wedges	2 tbsp	chili powder
		1/2 tsp	hot pepper flakes (optional)
1/2	red bell pepper, sliced	1/2 tsp	sea salt
1/2	medium green bell pepper, sliced	1/2 tsp	black pepper
		1	bay leaf
6	cloves garlic	7 cups	vegetable stock
		12 to 15	medium shrimp, peeled
		1/2 cup	chopped fresh parsley

Lightly spray a non-stick cookie sheet with vegetable cooking spray. Spread the carrots, zucchini, celery, onion, red pepper, green pepper and garlic on the cookie sheet and coat with vegetable spray. Broil or grill 8 to 10 minutes or until all vegetables are brown. Chop into bite-sized pieces. In a large soup pot, combine the stewed tomatoes and their juice, basil, sugar, chili powder, hot pepper flakes, salt, black pepper, bay leaf and stock. Bring to a boil; reduce heat and simmer for 10 minutes. Stir in the grilled vegetables, shrimp and parsley. Simmer another 5 minutes. Remove the bay leaf and serve.

Baby Shrimp Tomato Soup

This soup is too easy and delicious to pass up. Serve it with a pasta dish for a well-rounded meal.

Serves 6

Variation

Replace the shrimp with scallops or clams and cook in soup about 10 minutes.

1	28-oz can stewed tomatoes
1 cup	mild salsa
1	medium onion, chopped
2	cloves garlic, chopped
1 tbsp	sugar
1/2 tsp	dried basil
1/2 tsp	dried thyme
1/2 tsp	sea salt
1/2 tsp	black pepper
4 cups	vegetable stock
1/2 cup	red wine
1 cup	cooked baby shrimp
1/2 cup	chopped fresh coriander

In a large soup pot, combine the stewed tomatoes and their juice, salsa, onion, garlic, sugar, basil, thyme, salt, pepper, stock and wine. Bring to a boil; reduce heat and simmer for 10 minutes. Stir in shrimp and coriander and simmer until heated through.

Scallop Soup with Red Wine and Rosemary

Scallops with red wine and rosemary is an unusual
and inspired soup.

Serves 6

3 tbsp	unsalted butter
1	carrot, grated
4	shallots, chopped
2	cloves garlic, finely chopped
1 1/2 lb	medium or small scallops
1/2 cup	red wine
1/4 cup	chopped fresh basil
1 tbsp	chopped fresh rosemary
1 tbsp	Dijon mustard
1/2 tsp	sea salt
1/2 tsp	black pepper
1/4 tsp	hot pepper flakes
5 cups	fish stock
1/2 cup	table cream
1/4 cup	chopped fresh parsley

In a large soup pot, melt the butter. Add the carrot, shallots and garlic; sauté for 4 minutes or until shallots are translucent and carrot is tender. Add the scallops and sauté another 3 minutes. Add the wine and allow the liquid to reduce by half. Add the basil, rosemary, mustard, salt, pepper, hot pepper flakes and stock. Simmer 10 minutes. Stir in the cream and parsley. Serve immediately.

Squid Soup with Roasted Garlic and Sage

If you've never tried squid, here's your chance. This soup is a great introduction to one of the sea's tastiest cephalopods.

Serves 6

2 tbsp	olive oil
2	stalks celery, chopped
1	carrot, shredded
1	small red bell pepper, chopped
4	medium shallots, chopped OR 1 medium red onion, chopped
2 cups	chopped squid
1/2 cup	dry white wine
20	cloves roasted garlic, chopped (see page 23)
1 tbsp	Dijon mustard
1/2 tsp	dried sage
1/2 tsp	dried basil
1/2 tsp	sea salt
1/2 tsp	black pepper
1	bay leaf
6 cups	fish stock
1/2 cup	chopped fresh parsley

In a large soup pot, heat the oil. Add the celery, carrot, red pepper and shallots; sauté 3 minutes or until shallots are translucent. Add the squid and sauté another 5 minutes. Add the wine; simmer for 4 minutes or until liquid is reduced by half. Add the garlic, mustard, sage, basil, salt, pepper, bay leaf and stock. Simmer for 15 minutes. Remove the bay leaf. Garnish with parsley before serving.

Chicken and Turkey Deelight

Homey Chicken Soup with Rice   126

Chicken Soup with Portobello Mushrooms and Red Wine   127

Chicken, Bean and Coriander Soup   128

Chicken Monterey Jack Soup with Salsa   129

Egg Drop Soup with Chicken and Cream   130

Cream of Chicken Soup with Sage   131

Hot and Sour Grilled Chicken Soup   132

Chicken and Lime Soup   133

Lemon Chicken Soup with Leek   134

Grilled Chicken and Coconut Milk Soup   135

Chicken Coconut Soup with Lemongrass and Fennel   136

Curried Chicken Soup with Apple   137

Mulligatawny   138

Oriental Chicken and Corn Soup   139

Eastern Chicken Soup with Raisins and Rosemary   140

Turkey Soup with Salsa and Mint   141

Very Easy Turkey Chili Soup   142

Quick-and-Easy Turkey Wild Rice Soup   143

Homey Chicken Soup with Rice

Although homey, this chicken soup is anything but plain.

Serves 6

2 cups	cubed leftover chicken
1/2 cup	white rice
2	carrots, shredded
2	stalks celery, chopped
1	onion, chopped
2	cloves garlic, chopped
1/2 tsp	dried basil
1/2 tsp	dried oregano
1/2 tsp	sea salt
1/2 tsp	black pepper
1	bay leaf
7 cups	chicken stock
1/4 cup	chopped fresh parsley

In a large soup pot, combine the chicken, rice, carrots, celery, onion, garlic, basil, oregano, salt, pepper, bay leaf and stock. Bring to a boil; reduce heat and simmer for 15 minutes or until the rice is cooked. Remove the bay leaf. Stir in the parsley and serve immediately.

Chicken Soup with Portobello Mushrooms and Red Wine

Without the lovely portobello, this is plain old chicken with mushrooms.
Do make the effort and try this—you'll love it.

Serves 6

2 tbsp	olive oil
2	skinless, boneless chicken breasts, cut into thin strips
2 cups	thinly sliced portobello mushrooms (stems removed)
1	medium onion, cut into thin strips
1	red bell pepper, cut into thin strips
1/2 cup	red wine
1	28-oz can stewed tomatoes, diced
1/4 cup	chopped fresh basil
1 tbsp	chopped fresh rosemary
1 tbsp	chopped fresh thyme
1/2 tsp	sea salt
1/2 tsp	black pepper
1	bay leaf
6 cups	chicken stock
1/2 cup	chopped fresh parsley

In a large soup pot, heat the olive oil. Sauté the chicken 4 to 5 minutes or until no longer pink. Add the mushrooms, onion and red pepper; sauté another 5 minutes. Add the wine and cook, stirring, for 3 minutes. Add the stewed tomatoes and their juice, basil, rosemary, thyme, salt, black pepper, bay leaf and stock; simmer for 10 minutes. Remove the bay leaf. Stir in the parsley and serve immediately.

Chicken, Bean and Coriander Soup

Coriander, otherwise known as cilantro, adds bite
to this chicken and bean classic.

Serves 6

2 tbsp	olive oil
1	medium onion, chopped
2	cloves garlic, chopped
1 cup	cubed cooked chicken
1 cup	cooked red kidney beans
1/2 cup	red wine
1 cup	mild salsa
1/2 tsp	dried basil
1/2 tsp	dried rosemary
1/2 tsp	sea salt
1/2 tsp	black pepper
5 cups	vegetable stock
1/4 cup	chopped fresh coriander

In a large soup pot, heat the oil. Sauté the onion and garlic for 3 minutes. Add the chicken, beans and red wine; simmer another 2 minutes. Add the salsa, basil, rosemary, salt, pepper and stock. Bring to a boil; reduce heat and simmer for 10 minutes. Stir in the coriander and serve immediately.

Variation

Replace the coriander with fresh parsley.

Chicken Monterey Jack Soup with Salsa

*This southern-inspired soup is best served—I think—
with grilled vegetables. Enjoy!*

Serves 6 to 8

3 tbsp	olive oil
1	stalk celery, chopped
1	medium red onion, chopped
2	cloves garlic, finely chopped
1/2 cup	grated carrot
1/2	red bell pepper, chopped
1/2 cup	red wine
2 cups	cubed cooked chicken
1 cup	mild to hot salsa
1 tbsp	Dijon mustard
1/2 tsp	chili powder
1/2 tsp	dried basil
1/2 tsp	sea salt
1/2 tsp	black pepper
7 cups	chicken stock
3/4 cup	shredded Monterey Jack cheese
1/4 cup	chopped fresh coriander

> **Variation**
> Replace the Monterey Jack cheese with stilton.

In a large soup pot, heat the oil. Add the celery, onion, garlic, carrot and pepper; sauté for 2 minutes. Add the wine and sauté another 2 minutes. Add the chicken, salsa, mustard, chili powder, basil, salt, black pepper and stock. Bring to a boil; reduce heat and simmer for 15 minutes. Add the cheese and stir until the cheese has melted, about 2 minutes. Garnish with coriander and serve immediately.

Egg Drop Soup with Chicken and Cream

Dropping in freshly beaten eggs enriches this soup and gives it a lovely lemon yellow colour.

Serves 6 to 8

Variation

Leave out the cream and add an extra cup of soup stock or 1 cup apple juice.

2 cups	cubed cooked chicken
1	small onion, chopped
2	cloves garlic, chopped
1/2	red bell pepper, chopped
1/4 cup	finely chopped fresh basil
1 tbsp	finely chopped fresh oregano
1 tbsp	Dijon mustard
1 tbsp	balsamic vinegar
1/2 tsp	salt
1/2 tsp	black pepper
6 cups	chicken stock
3	eggs, well beaten
1 cup	table cream
1/4 cup	chopped fresh chives

In a large soup pot, combine the chicken, onion, garlic, red pepper, basil, oregano, mustard, balsamic vinegar, salt, black pepper and stock. Bring to a boil; reduce heat and simmer 10 minutes. Pour in eggs and cook, stirring constantly, for 2 minutes so the eggs don't lump together. Stir in cream and chives and serve immediately.

Cream of Chicken Soup with Sage

The aromatic fresh sage is a wonderful herb to add to chicken soup;
it's the defining taste here.

Serves 6 to 8

2 tbsp	unsalted butter
2	stalks celery, chopped
2	carrots, shredded
1	small red onion, chopped
2	cloves garlic, finely chopped
2 cups	cubed cooked chicken
1/2 cup	thawed frozen or canned corn
1/4 cup	chopped fresh sage
1/2 tsp	dried basil
1/2 tsp	dried oregano
1/2 tsp	salt
1/2 tsp	white pepper
6 cups	chicken stock
1 cup	table cream
1/2 cup	chopped fresh parsley

LowFatOption

Replace butter with canola oil. Replace the table cream with skim milk. Use low-fat chicken stock. 142.6 cal.

In a large soup pot, melt the butter. Add the celery, carrots, onion and garlic; sauté for 3 minutes or until onion is translucent. Add the chicken, corn, sage, basil, oregano, salt, pepper and stock. Bring to a boil; reduce heat and simmer for 15 minutes. Stir in cream and simmer another 5 minutes or until heated through. Garnish with parsley and serve.

Hot and Sour Grilled Chicken Soup

I love hot and sour soup, especially this way, with grilled chicken.

Serves 6

6 cups	chicken or beef stock
2	carrots, julienned
2	cloves garlic, crushed
1 cup	chopped mushrooms
1/2 cup	apple juice
1/4 cup	light soy sauce
2 tbsp	dry sherry (optional)
2 tbsp	rice wine vinegar
1 tbsp	lemon juice
1 tsp	chopped fresh ginger
1 tsp	brown sugar
1 tsp	balsamic vinegar
1/2 tsp	dried basil
2	grilled chicken breasts, cut into bite-sized pieces
1 cup	table cream
1/4 cup	chopped fresh chives

LowFatOption

Replace brown sugar with a calorie-reduced liquid sweetener. Use a low-sodium/low-fat vegetable stock. Replace cream with skim milk.
160.0 cal.

In a large soup pot, bring the stock to a boil. Add carrots, garlic, mushrooms, apple juice, soy sauce, sherry, rice wine vinegar, lemon juice, ginger, brown sugar, balsamic vinegar and basil. Reduce heat and simmer, stirring occasionally, for 15 minutes or until vegetables are tender. Stir in the chicken and cream. Simmer another 5 minutes. Taste; if the soup requires a bit more sugar, add another 1/2 tsp. Serve soup sprinkled with chives.

Chicken and Lime Soup

You gotta love this soup: the combination of chicken and lime is a winner.

Serves 6

2 tbsp	olive oil
1	small onion, chopped
2	boneless chicken breasts, cut into bite-sized pieces
2	medium tomatoes, chopped
1	red bell pepper, chopped
1/2 cup	chopped fresh tarragon
	Juice and skins of 2 limes
1 tsp	lime zest
1 tsp	dried basil
1/2 tsp	hot pepper sauce OR hot pepper flakes
1/2 tsp	salt
1/2 tsp	black pepper
6 cups	chicken stock
1 tbsp	brown sugar
1 oz	ouzo (optional)

> ## Variation
> Replace the tarragon with fresh parsley.

In a large soup pot, heat the oil. Sauté the onion for 2 minutes. Add the chicken and sauté another 5 minutes. Add the tomatoes, red pepper, tarragon, lime juice and skins, lime zest, basil, hot pepper sauce, salt, black pepper and stock. Simmer for 15 minutes. Add more stock or water if the soup is too thick. Stir in the sugar and the ouzo. Remove the lime skins and serve immediately.

Lemon Chicken Soup with Leek

You'll love this lemony, leeky chicken soup, simmered with wine and spiced with basil, thyme and pepper.

Serves 6 to 8

Variation

Replace the chicken with turkey, shrimp or thinly sliced beef or mushrooms.

3 tbsp	unsalted butter
2 cups	thinly sliced leeks
1/2 cup	grated carrot
1	medium onion, chopped
1/2 cup	dry white wine
2 cups	cubed cooked chicken
1/2 tsp	dried basil
1/2 tsp	dried thyme
1/2 tsp	sea salt
1/2 tsp	black pepper
7 cups	chicken stock
1/2 cup	lemon juice
1 tbsp	sugar
1 tbsp	lemon zest
1/4 cup	chopped fresh parsley

In a large soup pot, melt the butter. Sauté the leeks, carrot and onion for 2 minutes. Add the wine and simmer another 2 minutes. Add the chicken, basil, thyme, salt, pepper and stock. Bring to a boil; reduce heat and simmer for 10 minutes. Stir in the lemon juice, sugar and lemon zest. Simmer another minute before stirring in the parsley. Serve immediately.

Grilled Chicken and Coconut Milk Soup

This recipe brings back fond memories of the What's for Dinner? *episode in which I donned a chicken outfit. It was ridiculous, but Mary Jo loved it.*

Serves 6

1	medium potato, cubed
1	small zucchini, diced (about 1 cup)
1/2 cup	chopped fresh tarragon
1/2	green onion, chopped
	Zest and juice of 2 limes
1/2 tsp	white pepper
1/2 tsp	salt
6 cups	chicken stock
2	boneless chicken breasts, grilled with lime and sliced
1 cup	unsweetened coconut milk
1 tbsp	sugar

> ## LowFatOption
> Use low-fat chicken stock. Replace coconut milk with 1/2 cup coconut milk and 1/2 cup skim milk. 239.3 cal.

In a large soup pot, combine the potato, zucchini, half of the tarragon, green onion, lime zest and juice, pepper, salt and stock. Bring to a boil; reduce heat and simmer for 15 minutes or until potato is tender. Stir in the chicken, coconut milk and sugar. Simmer another 5 minutes or until heated through. Stir in the remaining tarragon before serving.

> ## Variation
> Replace chicken breasts with turkey or 2 swordfish steaks.

Chicken Coconut Soup with Lemongrass and Fennel

*The coconut and lemongrass add more than a frisson
of Indonesian flavour to this tasty soup.*

Serves 6

2 tbsp	olive oil		1/2 tsp	dried thyme
1 cup	finely chopped fennel		1/2 tsp	salt
1	medium onion, chopped		1/2 tsp	black pepper
2	cloves garlic, finely chopped		1	bay leaf
2	stalks lemongrass, white part only		6 cups	chicken stock
1 tsp	lemon zest		1 cup	sweetened coconut milk
1/2 tsp	grated fresh ginger		2 tbsp	lemon juice
2 cups	cubed cooked chicken		2 tbsp	soy sauce
1/2 cup	finely chopped fresh coriander		2	green onions, finely chopped

In a large soup pot, heat the oil. Add the fennel, onion and garlic; sauté for 2 minutes. Add lemongrass, lemon zest and ginger; sauté another 2 minutes. Add the
chicken, half of the coriander, thyme, salt, pepper, bay leaf, stock, coconut milk,
lemon juice and soy sauce. Bring to a boil; reduce heat and simmer for 15 minutes. Remove the lemongrass and bay leaf. Stir in the green onions and remaining coriander. Serve immediately.

Curried Chicken Soup with Apple

*This curried chicken with apple soup is always
a crowd pleaser at any event.*

Serves 6

2 tbsp	olive oil
1	medium onion, chopped
2	cloves garlic, minced
2	apples, cored and chopped
1/2 cup	frozen peas
1 tbsp	mild curry powder
1/2 tsp	cumin
1/2 tsp	dried basil
1/2 tsp	black pepper
1/4 tsp	salt
1/4 tsp	ground nutmeg
1	bay leaf
6 cups	chicken stock
1 cup	apple juice
2 cups	cubed cooked chicken
1/2 cup	cooked rice
1/2 cup	chopped fresh coriander

> ## LowFatOption
> Replace olive oil with
> 1/4 cup low-sodium/
> low-fat vegetable
> stock for sautéing.
> 186.8 cal.

In a large soup pot, heat the oil. Sauté the onion and garlic for 2 minutes or until
the onion is translucent. Stir in the apples, peas, curry powder, cumin, basil, pepper, salt, nutmeg, bay leaf, stock and apple juice. Bring to a boil; reduce heat and
simmer, stirring occasionally, 20 minutes. If liquid reduces too much, add more
apple juice. Stir in the chicken and rice; simmer another 5 minutes or until
chicken is heated through. Remove the bay leaf. Stir in the coriander and serve
immediately.

Mulligatawny

*Mulligatawny (or chicken curry soup) is world renowned.
My version is quicker and easier than most, but it doesn't
compromise on flavour ... I promise.*

Serves 8

LowFatOption

Replace cream with
skim milk. Replace
olive oil with canola
oil. Use low-fat
chicken stock.
270.9 cal.

2 tbsp	olive oil	1/2 cup	rice
2	skinless, boneless	1 tbsp	curry powder
	chicken breasts	1/2 tsp	cinnamon
2	stalks celery, chopped	1/2 tsp	dried basil
1	small red onion, chopped	1/2 tsp	salt
2	cloves garlic, finely chopped	1/2 tsp	white pepper
2	apples, peeled, cored	1	bay leaf
	and chopped	6 cups	chicken stock
1	red bell pepper, chopped	1 cup	apple juice
1 tsp	grated fresh ginger	1 cup	table cream

In a large soup pot, heat the oil. Add the chicken breasts and cook until no longer
pink. Remove pot from heat. Cube the chicken and set aside. Return the pot to
the heat; add celery, onion and garlic and sauté for 3 minutes. Add the apples, red
pepper and ginger; sauté another 2 minutes. Add the cooked chicken, rice, curry
powder, cinnamon, basil, salt, white pepper, bay leaf, stock and apple juice. Bring
to a boil; reduce heat and simmer for 15 minutes. Stir in cream and simmer
another 5 minutes or until heated through. Remove the bay leaf before serving.

Oriental Chicken and Corn Soup

*It's the soy, ginger and bean sprouts that give this soup
its Asian pedigree.*

Serves 6 to 8

1/4 lb	bacon, chopped
1 tbsp	olive oil
1	medium onion, chopped
4	cloves garlic, chopped
6 cups	beef stock
1/4 cup	soy sauce
1 tbsp	finely chopped fresh ginger
1 tbsp	lemon juice
1/2 tsp	dried basil
1/2 tsp	black pepper
1	bay leaf
2	eggs, well beaten
2 cups	cubed cooked chicken
2 cups	creamed corn
1/2 cup	bean sprouts (optional)
1/2 cup	chopped green onion

In a large soup pot, cook the bacon until nearly crisp. Remove and drain on a paper towel. Drain all bacon fat. In the same pot, heat the olive oil. Sauté the onion and garlic for 2 minutes. Add the stock, soy sauce, ginger, lemon juice, basil, pepper and bay leaf. Bring to a boil; reduce heat and simmer for 5 minutes. Add the eggs and stir well; simmer another 10 minutes. Stir in the chicken, creamed corn and bean sprouts; simmer another 5 minutes. Remove the bay leaf. Serve garnished with green onions and bacon.

Eastern Chicken Soup with Raisins and Rosemary

With raisins and couscous, this soup is more Moroccan than oriental; but it's all really a matter of perspective.

Serves 4 to 6

LowFatOption

Replace olive oil with 1/4 cup low-fat chicken stock for sautéing. Replace chicken stock with low-fat chicken stock.
185.8 cal.

2 tbsp	olive oil
1	medium onion, chopped
1/2	green bell pepper, chopped
1/2	red bell pepper, chopped
6 cups	chicken stock
1/2 cup	apple juice
1 tsp	dried rosemary
1/2 tsp	salt
1/2 tsp	black pepper
1	bay leaf
2 cups	cubed cooked chicken
1/4 cup	couscous
1/4 cup	raisins
1/4 cup	chopped fresh parsley

In a large soup pot, heat the oil. Gently sauté the onion and peppers for 2 minutes. Add the stock, apple juice, rosemary, salt, black pepper and bay leaf. Bring to a boil; reduce heat and simmer for 5 minutes. Stir in the chicken, couscous and raisins; simmer another 5 minutes. Remove the bay leaf. Stir in the parsley and serve immediately.

Turkey Soup with Salsa and Mint

Next to chicken, turkey is my favourite bird. This salsa-mint combo
should be retitled Turkey Delight.

Serves 6 to 8

3 tbsp	olive oil
2	stalks celery, chopped
1	medium onion, chopped
2	cloves garlic, chopped
1/2	green bell pepper, chopped
1/2 cup	grated carrot
1	28-oz can stewed tomatoes, diced
1 cup	mild to hot salsa
1/2 tsp	chili powder
1/2 tsp	dried basil
1/2 tsp	dried sage
1/2 tsp	sea salt
1/2 tsp	black pepper
6 cups	chicken stock
2 1/2 cups	cubed cooked turkey
1/4 cup	finely chopped fresh mint

> ### Variation
> Replace the mint with parsley. Add 1/2 cup red wine.

In a large soup pot, heat the oil. Add the celery, onion, garlic, green pepper and carrot; sauté for 2 minutes. Add the stewed tomatoes and their juice, salsa, chili powder, basil, sage, salt, pepper and stock. Bring to a boil; reduce heat and simmer 10 minutes. Add the turkey and mint. Simmer for another 5 minutes and serve.

Very Easy Turkey Chili Soup

This is a great meal, and perfect for leftover turkey.

Serves 6

7 cups	chicken stock
1	28-oz can stewed tomatoes, diced
1 cup	mild to hot salsa
1 cup	mashed potatoes
1	carrot, grated
1	red bell pepper, chopped
1	small onion, chopped
1/2 cup	chopped fresh coriander
2 tbsp	chili powder
1/2 tsp	dried basil
1/2 tsp	dried oregano
1/2 tsp	dried thyme
1/2 tsp	salt
1/2 tsp	black pepper
1	bay leaf
1/2 cup	cooked red kidney beans
1 cup	cooked turkey cut into pieces
1/4 cup	sour cream

> **Variation**
>
> Add any leftover vegetables you have in the fridge.

In a large soup pot, bring the stock to a boil. Add the stewed tomatoes and their juice, salsa, mashed potatoes, carrot, red pepper, onion, half of the coriander, chili powder, basil, oregano, thyme, salt, black pepper and bay leaf. Simmer for 10 minutes. Add the kidney beans, turkey, and remaining coriander; simmer another 5 minutes. Remove the bay leaf. Serve immediately garnished with sour cream.

Quick-and-Easy Turkey Wild Rice Soup

Although this recipe does call for wild rice, which gives it a terrific nutty flavour, you could substitute any other kind of rice.

Serves 6

1	28-oz can stewed tomatoes, diced	1 cup	chopped cooked turkey
7 cups	chicken or turkey stock	1/2 cup	frozen peas
1/2 cup	wild rice	1/4 cup	chopped fresh basil
2	medium carrots, chopped	2 tbsp	Dijon mustard
2	stalks celery, chopped	1 tbsp	chopped fresh sage
1	small green bell pepper, chopped	1 tbsp	chopped fresh thyme
1	medium onion, chopped	1 tbsp	balsamic vinegar
2	cloves garlic, finely chopped	1/2 tsp	sea salt
		1/2 tsp	black pepper
		1	bay leaf

In a large soup pot, combine the stewed tomatoes and their juice and the stock; bring to a boil. Add the wild rice; boil for 5 minutes, then reduce heat to a simmer. Add the carrots, celery, green pepper, onion, garlic, turkey, peas, basil, mustard, sage, thyme, balsamic vinegar, salt, black pepper and bay leaf. Simmer for 15 minutes or until the rice is cooked. Remove the bay leaf and serve immediately.

The Beef, the Bacon and the Wee Lamb

Beef and Apple Cinnamon Soup   146

Beef Barley Soup with Red Wine and Roasted Garlic   147

Creamy Beef and Egg Noodle Soup   148

Meatball and Parmesan Egg Noodle Soup   149

Hamburger Parmesan Soup   150

Pepperpot with Blue Cheese   151

Spicy Beef Soup with Salsa and Sun-Dried Tomato   152

Grilled Beef Steak and Vegetable Soup   153

Bacon and Potato Cheese Soup   154

Bacon and Chick Pea Soup with Herbs   155

Bacon, Celery and Spicy Tomato Soup   156

Bacon, Cabbage and Apple Soup   157

Portobello Mushroom, Barley and Grilled Pork Soup   158

Curried Pork Soup with Apple and Chutney   159

Lamb, Feta and Rosemary Rice Soup   160

Lamb, Apricot and Ginger Soup   161

Sausage and Chicken Gumbo   162

Sausage Split Pea Soup with Dijon   163

Beef and Apple Cinnamon Soup

This savoury and sweet combination is one of my favourite soups.

Serves 6

Variation

Replace apples with pears, omit the cinnamon and stir in 1/4 cup crumbled stilton or blue cheese just before serving.

2 tbsp	olive oil
1 lb	lean ground beef
1	medium onion, chopped
1/2 cup	red wine
2	apples, peeled, cored and cubed
1 tbsp	Worcestershire sauce
1 tsp	horseradish (optional)
1/2 tsp	chili powder
1/2 tsp	cinnamon
1/2 tsp	dried basil
1/2 tsp	dried thyme
1/2 tsp	sea salt
1/2 tsp	black pepper
4 cups	beef stock
2 cups	apple juice

In a large soup pot, heat the oil. Sauté the ground beef for 5 minutes or until no longer pink. Add the onion and sauté another 2 minutes. Add the wine and allow the liquid to reduce by half. Add the apples, Worcestershire sauce, horseradish, chili powder, cinnamon, basil, thyme, salt, pepper, stock and apple juice. Bring to a boil; reduce heat and simmer for 10 minutes. Serve immediately.

Beef Barley Soup with Red Wine and Roasted Garlic

If you don't have a terra cotta garlic roaster, seal unpeeled garlic cloves in aluminum foil and bake at 350°F for 20 minutes. When they're done, the skins will come off easily.

Serves 6

2 tbsp	olive oil
1 lb	stewing beef, cut into bite-sized pieces
2	medium carrots, grated
1	red bell pepper, chopped
1	medium onion, chopped
10	cloves roasted garlic, chopped
1/2 cup	red wine
1	28-oz can stewed tomatoes
6 cups	beef stock
1/2 cup	barley
1/2 cup	chopped fresh basil
1 tbsp	chopped fresh thyme
1 tbsp	Worcestershire sauce
1 tbsp	horseradish
1/2 tsp	sea salt
1/2 tsp	black pepper

Variation

Replace the beef with lamb or pork.

In a large soup pot, heat the oil. Add the beef, carrots, red pepper and onion; sauté for 4 minutes or until beef is browned. Add the roasted garlic and wine; sauté until the liquid has evaporated, 2 to 3 minutes. Add the tomatoes and their juice, stock, barley, basil, thyme, Worcestershire sauce, horseradish, salt and black pepper. Bring to a boil; reduce heat and simmer another 10 to 12 minutes or until the barley is tender. Serve immediately.

Creamy Beef and Egg Noodle Soup

For me, this is the perfect comfort-food soup.

Serves 6

2 tbsp	olive oil
1 lb	lean ground beef
2	stalks celery, chopped
2	medium carrots, chopped or shredded
1	medium onion, chopped
1	small green bell pepper, chopped
1 cup	red wine
5 cups	beef stock
1 tbsp	Dijon mustard
1 tsp	Worcestershire sauce
1/2 tsp	dried basil
1/2 tsp	dried oregano
1/2 tsp	dried thyme
1/2 tsp	sea salt
1/2 tsp	black pepper
1 cup	egg noodles
1 cup	table cream

In a large soup pot, heat the oil. Add the beef and gently sauté for 5 minutes or until browned. Add the celery, carrots, onion and green pepper; sauté another 5 minutes. Add the red wine; allow to reduce another 5 minutes. Add the stock, mustard, Worcestershire sauce, basil, oregano, thyme, salt and black pepper. Bring to a boil; reduce heat and simmer for 10 minutes. Stir in the egg noodles and cream. Simmer until noodles are cooked, about 5 minutes. Serve immediately.

Meatball and Parmesan Egg Noodle Soup

Although I've given you a lovely, simple recipe for meatballs here, you can always take a shortcut and toss in the already-prepared kind.

Serves 6

	Meatballs			**Soup**
1 lb	lean ground beef		2 tbsp	olive oil
1/4 cup	fine dry bread crumbs		2	stalks celery, chopped
1/2 tsp	onion powder		1	small green bell pepper, chopped
1/2 tsp	garlic powder		1	medium onion, chopped
1/2 tsp	dried basil		1/2 cup	grated carrot
1 tbsp	olive oil		2	cloves garlic, finely chopped
			1	28-oz can stewed tomatoes, diced
			1 tbsp	chili powder
			1/2 tsp	dried basil
			1/2 tsp	dried oregano
			1/2 tsp	sea salt
			1/2 tsp	black pepper
			1	bay leaf
			5 cups	beef stock
			1/2 cup	narrow egg noodles
			1/4 cup	grated Parmesan cheese

To make the meatballs, combine the beef, bread crumbs, onion powder, garlic powder and basil. Shape into bite-sized meatballs. In a sauté pan, heat the oil. Fry the meatballs, shaking frequently, until brown on all sides. Set aside.

In a large soup pot, heat the oil. Sauté the celery, green pepper, onion, carrot and garlic for 3 minutes. Add the stewed tomatoes and their juice, chili powder, basil, oregano, salt, black pepper, bay leaf and stock. Bring to a boil; reduce heat and simmer for 10 minutes. Stir in the egg noodles and simmer another 3 to 4 minutes or until noodles are cooked. Remove the bay leaf. Stir in the Parmesan and serve immediately.

Hamburger Parmesan Soup

This hamburger soup is a one-pot meal. Be sure to buy lean ground beef and be aware that 1 teaspoon of Parmesan cheese has 2 grams of fat.

Serves 4 to 6

Variation

Replace lean ground beef with lean ground chicken or turkey. Replace beef stock with chicken stock.

3 tbsp	olive oil
2	stalks celery, finely chopped
1	green bell pepper, chopped
1	medium onion, chopped
2	cloves garlic, chopped
1/2 lb	very lean ground beef
4	plum tomatoes, chopped
1/2 tsp	dried basil
1/2 tsp	dried rosemary
6 cups	beef stock
1/4 cup	red wine
1/2 cup	grated Parmesan cheese

In a large soup pot, heat the oil. Add the celery, green pepper, onion and garlic; sauté for 2 minutes or until the onion is translucent. Add the ground beef and sauté until browned. Add the tomatoes, basil, rosemary, stock and wine; simmer for 15 minutes. If the soup reduces too much, add more beef stock. Stir in the Parmesan cheese and serve immediately.

LowFatOption

Replace olive oil with canola oil. Replace the lean ground beef with lean ground turkey. Use low-fat beef stock. Use low-fat Parmesan cheese.
208.6 cal.

Pepperpot with Blue Cheese

*The mild mint and blue cheese combo will set
your taste buds tap dancing!*

Serves 4

2 tbsp	olive oil
2 lb	cubed lean beef
1	medium onion, chopped
2	cloves garlic, finely chopped
2	red bell peppers, chopped
1	green bell pepper, chopped
1 cup	cubed squash
2	hot peppers, chopped
1 tsp	chopped fresh oregano
1 tsp	cayenne pepper
1/4 tsp	cinnamon
	Salt and black pepper to taste
6 cups	vegetable stock
1/2 cup	crumbled blue cheese
1/4 cup	chopped fresh coriander

LowFatOption

Replace beef with
cubed turkey. Replace
olive oil with 1/4 cup
vegetable stock for
sautéing.
518.7 cal.

In a large soup pot, heat the oil. Add the beef and sauté until browned. Remove beef and set aside. Add the onion and garlic; sauté for 2 minutes or until the onion is translucent. Add the red peppers, green pepper and squash; sauté for 2 minutes. Add the hot peppers, oregano, cayenne, cinnamon, salt, black pepper, cooked beef and stock. Bring to a boil; reduce heat and simmer for 15 to 20 minutes or until vegetables are tender. Five minutes before serving, stir in the blue cheese and coriander.

Variation

Replace the blue
cheese with stilton.

Spicy Beef Soup with Salsa and Sun-Dried Tomato

This is a perfect soup to serve with hot tamales, warm tortillas or cool refried beans.

Serves 6

1 cup	sun-dried tomatoes
2 tbsp	olive oil
2	stalks celery, chopped
1	small red bell pepper, chopped
1	medium onion, chopped
2	cloves garlic, finely chopped
1 lb	round steak, cut into bite-sized pieces
1	28-oz can stewed tomatoes, diced
1 cup	hot salsa
1/2 cup	chopped fresh coriander
1/2 cup	chopped fresh parsley
1 tsp	hot pepper sauce (optional)
1/2 tsp	sea salt
1/2 tsp	black pepper
1	bay leaf
6 cups	beef stock

Rehydrate the sun-dried tomatoes in hot water; drain, chop and set aside. In a large soup pot, heat the oil. Sauté the celery, red pepper, onion and garlic for 2 minutes. Add the beef and sauté another 5 minutes. Add the stewed tomatoes and their juice, sun-dried tomatoes, salsa, half of the coriander, half of the parsley, hot pepper sauce, salt, black pepper, bay leaf and stock. Bring to a boil; reduce heat and simmer for 15 minutes. Remove the bay leaf. Stir in the remaining coriander and parsley and serve immediately.

Grilled Beef Steak and Vegetable Soup

If you haven't got a T-bone steak, substitute with another cut,
but do try to grill the meat before adding it to the soup.

Serves 6 to 8

2 tbsp	olive oil		1 cup	frozen broccoli
1	medium red onion, chopped		2 tbsp	Dijon mustard
2	cloves garlic, chopped		1 tbsp	Worcestershire sauce
1 lb	grilled beef steak (round,		1/2 tsp	dried basil
	T-bone or New York),		1/2 tsp	dried oregano
	thinly sliced		1/2 tsp	dried sage
1/2 cup	red wine (optional)		1/2 tsp	sea salt
1	medium potato, peeled		1/2 tsp	black pepper
	and cubed		1	bay leaf
1 cup	frozen peas		7 cups	beef stock
1 cup	frozen corn		1/2 cup	chopped fresh parsley
1 cup	frozen carrots		1 tbsp	horseradish (optional)

In a large soup pot, heat the oil. Sauté the onion and garlic for 3 minutes or until onion is translucent. Add the grilled steak and wine, if using; simmer for 3 minutes. Add the potato, peas, corn, carrots, broccoli, mustard, Worcestershire sauce, basil, oregano, sage, salt, pepper, bay leaf and stock. Bring to a boil; reduce heat and simmer for 10 minutes. Remove the bay leaf. Stir in the parsley and horseradish, if using, and serve immediately.

Bacon and Potato Cheese Soup

The great thing about this soup is that it's delicious and easy;
you probably have most of the ingredients—if not all of them—
in your fridge.

Serves 6 to 8

1/2 lb	bacon, diced		1/2 tsp	dried basil
1	large onion, chopped		8 cups	chicken stock
2	cloves garlic, chopped		1 cup	shredded cheddar cheese
4	large potatoes, peeled and cubed		1/2 cup	table cream
			1/2 cup	milk
1 tsp	black pepper		1/4 cup	chopped fresh parsley
1/2 tsp	salt			

> ### Variation
> For a completely different soup, replace the potato with sweet potato and add 1/2 tsp mild curry powder and 1/2 tsp cinnamon.

In a large soup pot, sauté the bacon until cooked but not crisp. Add the onion and garlic; sauté for 2 minutes. Drain off any excess fat. Add the potatoes, pepper, salt, basil and stock. Bring to a boil; reduce heat and simmer for 15 minutes or until potatoes are cooked. Using a hand blender, puree the soup until smooth. Stir in the cheese, cream and milk. Simmer, stirring, another 3 to 5 minutes or until cheese has melted. Garnish with parsley and serve.

> ### Low**Fat**Option
> Replace bacon with turkey or chicken bacon. Replace cream with non-fat sour cream. Replace milk with skim milk. Use low-fat cheddar cheese. Use low-fat chicken stock.
> 155.2 cal.

Bacon and Chick Pea Soup with Herbs

I love to use bacon in my soup recipes. The bacon and chick pea combination makes this soup more than worth the effort.

Serves 4 to 6

1/4 lb	bacon, chopped
1	small onion, chopped
2	cloves garlic, chopped
2	plum tomatoes, chopped
6 cups	chicken stock
1/4 cup	chopped fresh basil OR 1/2 tsp dried
1/4 cup	chopped fresh oregano OR 1/2 tsp dried
1/2 tsp	chili powder
1/2 tsp	salt
1/2 tsp	black pepper
2 cups	cooked chick peas
1/4 cup	finely chopped fresh dill

In a large soup pot, fry the bacon until cooked but not crisp. Add the onion and garlic; sauté another 2 minutes. Stir in tomatoes, stock, basil, oregano, chili powder, salt and pepper; simmer for 10 minutes. Add chick peas and simmer another 5 minutes. Garnish with dill and serve.

Variation
Replace chick peas with cooked black, white or kidney beans.

LowFatOption
Replace bacon with turkey or chicken bacon. Use low-fat chicken stock. 307.6 cal.

Bacon, Celery and Spicy Tomato Soup

Since this recipe calls for lean bacon, you might want to try turkey bacon; the soup will taste just as delicious.

Serves 6

1/4 lb	lean bacon, chopped	1 tbsp	balsamic vinegar
2 tbsp	olive oil	1 tsp	finely chopped jalapeno
2 cups	chopped celery		pepper
1	medium onion, chopped	1/2 tsp	hot pepper flakes
4	medium tomatoes, chopped	1/2 tsp	dried basil
1/2 cup	red wine	1/2 tsp	dried oregano
1	28-oz can stewed tomatoes, diced	1/2 tsp	sea salt
		1/2 tsp	black pepper
2 tbsp	Dijon mustard	1	bay leaf
1 tbsp	sugar	6 cups	beef stock
1 tbsp	chili powder		

In a large soup pot, fry the bacon for 4 to 5 minutes or until tender, not crisp. Remove and drain on a paper towel. Remove fat from pot, add the olive oil and sauté the celery and onion for 4 minutes. Add the chopped tomatoes and wine; simmer for 5 minutes. Add the stewed tomatoes and their juice, mustard, sugar, chili powder, balsamic vinegar, jalapeno pepper, hot pepper flakes, basil, oregano, salt, black pepper, bay leaf and stock. Simmer for 5 minutes. Add the bacon; simmer another 5 minutes. Remove bay leaf and serve immediately.

Bacon, Cabbage and Apple Soup

*Although this recipe screams "FALL," it's so delicious
I have it all year round.*

Serves 6

1/4 lb	bacon, chopped
2 tbsp	olive oil
2 cups	chopped cabbage
1	medium onion, chopped
2	apples, peeled, cored and cubed
1 tbsp	Dijon mustard
1/2 tsp	cinnamon
1/2 tsp	dried basil
1/2 tsp	dried oregano
1/2 tsp	sea salt
1/2 tsp	black pepper
5 cups	vegetable stock
1 cup	apple juice
1/4 cup	chopped fresh parsley

> Variation
>
> Replace bacon with 1/2 lb chicken or turkey bacon.

In a large soup pot, sauté the bacon until tender, not crisp. Remove and drain on a paper towel. Drain off the fat. In the same pot, heat the oil. Sauté the cabbage and onion for 5 minutes. Add the apples, mustard, cinnamon, basil, oregano, salt, pepper, stock and apple juice. Bring to a boil; reduce heat, add the bacon and simmer for 10 minutes. Serve garnished with parsley.

Portobello Mushroom, Barley and Grilled Pork Soup

*If you haven't got a portobello, another mushroom will do—
but try for something interesting, like a shiitake.*

Serves 6

2 tbsp	olive oil
1	medium onion, chopped
1	small red bell pepper, chopped
1 cup	chopped portobello mushrooms (stems removed)
1/2 cup	red wine
6 cups	beef stock
1 cup	apple juice
1/2 cup	barley
1/4 cup	chopped fresh basil
1 tbsp	chopped fresh rosemary
1 tbsp	chopped fresh thyme
1 lb	pork tenderloin, grilled and sliced
1/4 cup	chopped fresh parsley

In a large soup pot, heat the oil. Add the onion, red pepper and mushrooms; sauté for 5 minutes or until the pepper is tender. Add the wine, stock, apple juice, barley, basil, rosemary and thyme. Bring to a boil; reduce heat and simmer for 10 minutes. Add the pork tenderloin and simmer another 2 minutes. Garnish with parsley and serve immediately.

Curried Pork Soup with Apple and Chutney

This soup has more than a hint of the "time of the Raj"—the British empire-builders were so fond of the flavours of curry and chutney in India that they brought those flavours home with them.

Serves 6

2 tbsp	olive oil	1 cup	apple juice
1 lb	lean pork (tenderloin, chop, steak), trimmed of fat, thinly sliced	1/2 cup	applesauce
		1/2 cup	basmati or white rice
		1/2 tsp	dried basil
1	medium red onion, chopped	1/2 tsp	sea salt
1	small red bell pepper, chopped	1/2 tsp	black pepper
		2	apples, peeled, cored and diced
2	cloves garlic, finely chopped		
1	medium potato, peeled and cubed	1/2 cup	raisins
		1/2 cup	chutney
1 tbsp	mild curry powder	1/2 tsp	cinnamon
6 cups	vegetable stock	1/2 cup	chopped fresh coriander

In a large soup pot, heat the oil. Add the pork, onion, red pepper and garlic; sauté for 5 minutes or until the pepper is tender and pork is no longer pink. Add the potato and curry powder and stir briefly. Add the stock, apple juice, applesauce, rice, basil, salt and black pepper. Bring to a boil; reduce heat and simmer for 10 minutes. Stir in the apples, raisins, chutney and cinnamon; simmer another 5 minutes. Stir in the coriander and serve.

Lamb, Feta and Rosemary Rice Soup

This is an inspired soup: the feta cheese and rosemary make all the difference here.

Serves 6

2 tbsp	olive oil
1 lb	lean stewing lamb, cut into bite-sized pieces
1	medium red onion, chopped
1	small red bell pepper, chopped
1 cup	red wine
6 cups	beef stock
1/2 cup	white rice
1/2 cup	chopped fresh parsley
2 tbsp	chopped fresh rosemary
1/2 tsp	dried basil
1/2 tsp	dried oregano
1/2 tsp	salt
1/2 tsp	black pepper
1	bay leaf
1/2 cup	crumbled feta cheese

In a large soup pot, heat the oil. Add the lamb and sauté for 5 minutes or until no longer pink. Add the onion and red pepper; sauté another 4 minutes. Add the wine and simmer for 5 minutes. Add the stock, rice, half of the parsley, rosemary, basil, oregano, salt, black pepper and bay leaf; simmer for 10 minutes. Remove the bay leaf. Stir in the feta cheese and the remaining parsley. Serve immediately.

Lamb, Apricot and Ginger Soup

*Fresh ginger and dried apricots are a dynamite
combination with lamb.*

Serves 6

2 tbsp	olive oil
1 lb	stewing lamb, cut into bite-sized pieces
1 tbsp	flour
1	medium onion, chopped
2	cloves garlic, chopped
1	28-oz can stewed tomatoes
1	potato, cubed
1 cup	dried apricots
1 tsp	grated fresh ginger
1 tsp	dried rosemary
1/2 tsp	dried basil
1/2 tsp	salt
1/2 tsp	black pepper
1	bay leaf
6 cups	beef stock
1 cup	red wine
1/4 cup	chopped fresh parsley

LowFatOption

Replace olive oil with
canola oil. Use low-
fat beef stock.
365.6 cal.

In a large soup pot, heat the oil. Coat the lamb with flour; add it to the pot and
brown for 4 minutes, stirring frequently. Add the onion and garlic; sauté for 2
minutes. Add the stewed tomatoes and their juice, potato, apricots, ginger, rosemary, basil, salt, pepper, bay leaf, stock and wine. Bring to a boil; reduce heat and
simmer for 15 minutes. Remove the bay leaf. Garnish with parsley and serve.

Sausage and Chicken Gumbo

In case you were wondering, this chicken-sausage gumbo is definitely a one-pot meal. Keep it simple and serve piping hot!

Serves 6

1/4 cup plus 2 tbsp	olive oil
1/2 cup	flour
4	stalks celery, chopped
1	green bell pepper, chopped
1	medium onion, chopped
2	cloves garlic, finely chopped
1	small jalapeno pepper, diced
2 cups	cubed cooked chicken
2	mild Italian sausages, cooked and chopped
6 cups	chicken stock
1/2 cup	dry white wine (optional)
1/2 cup	white rice
1/2 tsp	dried basil
1/2 tsp	dried oregano
1/2 tsp	paprika
1/2 tsp	chili powder
1/2 tsp	salt
1/2 tsp	black pepper
1	bay leaf

In a sauté pan, heat 1/4 cup of the oil over medium-low heat. Gradually stir in the flour, and stir constantly for 10 minutes or until the roux turns brown. Immediately remove from the heat. In a large soup pot, heat the remaining 2 tbsp oil. Sauté the celery, green pepper and onion for 3 minutes. Stir in the roux, garlic, jalapeno pepper, chicken, sausages, stock and wine, if using. Bring to a boil, stirring; reduce heat to a simmer. Stir in the rice, basil, oregano, paprika, chili powder, salt, black pepper and bay leaf. Simmer for 12 to 15 minutes or until the rice is cooked. Remove the bay leaf and serve immediately.

Sausage Split Pea Soup with Dijon

Split pea soup is a staple for me; try my Dijon version and let me know what you think!

Serves 8

2 tbsp	olive oil
1	medium red onion, chopped
2	cloves garlic, finely chopped
2 cups	split peas
8 cups	vegetable or chicken stock
1/2 tsp	dried basil
1/2 tsp	dried sage
1/2 tsp	dried oregano
1/2 tsp	salt
1/2 tsp	white pepper
1	bay leaf
1 cup	table cream
1/4 cup	Dijon mustard
2	cooked medium Italian sausages, sliced
1/2 cup	chopped fresh parsley

LowFatOption

Replace the olive oil with canola oil. Use low-fat vegetable stock. Replace cream with skim milk. 190.0 cal.

In a large soup pot, heat the oil. Add the onion and garlic; sauté for 2 to 3 minutes or until the onion is translucent. Add the split peas, stock, basil, sage, oregano, salt, pepper and bay leaf. Bring to a boil; reduce heat and simmer for 25 minutes or until split peas are cooked. Remove the bay leaf. Using a hand blender, puree the soup until smooth. Stir in the cream, mustard and sausages. Simmer another 5 minutes or until heated through. Garnish with parsley and serve.

Haute, Haute, Haute

Cream of Garlic Soup with Capers   166

Roasted Garlic and Wild Rice Soup with Fresh Basil   167

Pearl Onion Soup with White Wine and Coriander   168

Blue Cheese Celery Soup   169

White Asparagus Soup with White Wine and Fresh Herbs   170

Artichoke and Prosciutto Soup with White Wine and Stilton   171

Avocado and Salsa Soup with Fresh Herbs   172

Zucchini and Red Pepper Soup with Red Wine and Salsa   173

Carrot and Orange Mint Soup   174

Cream of Carrot Soup with Grand Marnier and Orange   175

Cream of Escargot Soup with Port   176

Cream of Shrimp Soup with Orange Liqueur   177

Smoked Salmon Soup with Baby Shrimp and Vodka   178

Crabmeat Bisque with Dill   179

Lobster Curry Soup   180

Four Cheese Soup with Lobster and Fresh Herbs   181

Lobster Stew with Cognac and Fresh Sage   182

Steak and Lobster Soup with Red Wine and Fresh Herbs   183

Mussel Soup with Coconut Milk and Pernod   184

Frogs' Leg Soup with White Wine and Fresh Rosemary   185

Cream of Garlic Soup with Capers

Cream of garlic! Who would have thought …

Serves 6

LowFatOption

Leave out the butter.
Replace olive oil with
canola oil. Replace
cream with skim milk.
Use low-fat vegetable
stock.
137.8 cal.

2 tbsp	olive oil
1 tbsp	unsalted butter
10	cloves garlic, chopped
4	shallots, chopped
2	potatoes, peeled and cubed
1/4 cup	dry white wine
6 cups	vegetable stock
1 tbsp	chopped fresh thyme
1 tbsp	chopped fresh oregano
1/2 tsp	salt
1/2 tsp	white pepper
1 cup	table cream
1/2 cup	capers
1/4 cup	chopped fresh parsley

In a large soup pot, heat the oil and butter. Sauté the garlic and shallots for 3 minutes. Add the potatoes and wine; sauté another 2 minutes, allowing the wine to reduce. Add the stock, thyme, oregano, salt and pepper. Bring to a boil; reduce the heat and simmer for 10 minutes. Using a hand blender, puree the soup till smooth. Stir in the cream and capers; heat through if necessary. Serve garnished with parsley.

Roasted Garlic and Wild Rice Soup with Fresh Basil

This is divine because it calls for 25 roasted garlic cloves.

Serves 6

25	cloves garlic
2 tbsp	unsalted butter
1	apple, peeled, cored and cubed
1	small potato, peeled and cubed
1	small red bell pepper, chopped
4	shallots, chopped
5 cups	vegetable stock
1 cup	apple juice
1/2 cup	dry white wine
1/2 cup	chopped fresh basil
1/2 tsp	dried thyme
1/2 tsp	salt
1/2 tsp	black pepper
1/4 tsp	cinnamon
1	bay leaf
1/2 cup	wild rice

Place peeled garlic cloves on a cookie sheet and spray with vegetable oil. Bake at 350°F for 20 minutes or until golden; be careful not to burn. In a large soup pot, melt the butter. Add the apple, potato, red pepper and shallots; sauté for 3 minutes. Add the roasted garlic, stock, apple juice, wine, half the basil, thyme, salt, black pepper, cinnamon and bay leaf. Bring to a boil; reduce heat and simmer for 10 minutes. Remove bay leaf. Using a hand blender, puree the soup until it is smooth. Add the wild rice and simmer another 15 minutes or until rice is cooked. If the soup thickens, add more stock or apple juice. Stir in remaining basil just before serving.

Pearl Onion Soup with White Wine and Coriander

This soup is a veritable treasure trove of pearls and spices.

Serves 6

6 cups	vegetable stock
1 cup	dry white wine
1	red bell pepper, chopped
2	cloves garlic, chopped
1/2 cup	chopped fresh coriander
1 tbsp	chopped fresh basil
1 tbsp	Dijon mustard
1 tbsp	lemon juice
1/2 tsp	dried thyme
1/2 tsp	salt
1/2 tsp	white pepper
1	bay leaf
3 cups	pearl onions
1/4 cup	Port

In a large soup pot, bring the stock and wine to a boil; reduce heat to a simmer. Add the red pepper, garlic, half of the coriander, basil, mustard (mix in well), lemon juice, thyme, salt, white pepper and bay leaf; simmer for 10 minutes. Add the pearl onions and Port; simmer another 5 minutes. Remove the bay leaf. Using a hand blender, puree the soup till smooth. Serve garnished with the remaining coriander.

Blue Cheese Celery Soup

*Don't let the title fool you: although this soup stars the lovely
lithe celery and the nippy blue cheese, it includes
a stellar cast of characters.*

Serves 6

3 tbsp	unsalted butter	1 tbsp	chopped fresh thyme
10	stalks celery, chopped	1 tbsp	chopped fresh oregano
1	medium red onion, chopped	1/2 tsp	salt
1	small green bell pepper, chopped	1/2 tsp	white pepper
		1	bay leaf
2	medium potatoes, peeled and cubed	6 cups	vegetable stock
1/2 cup	dry white wine	1/2 cup	crumbled blue cheese
1/4 cup	chopped fresh basil	1/2 cup	table cream

Variation

Replace celery with fennel.

In a large soup pot, melt the butter. Sauté the celery, onion and green pepper for 3 minutes. Add the potatoes and wine; simmer for 3 minutes or until the wine reduces by half. Add the basil, thyme, oregano, salt, white pepper, bay leaf and stock. Bring to a boil; reduce heat and simmer for 5 minutes. Remove the bay leaf. Add blue cheese and cream; simmer, stirring, until heated through—do not boil. Serve immediately.

LowFatOption

Replace cream with skim milk. Replace blue cheese with light feta. Use low-fat vegetable stock.
183.5 cal.

White Asparagus Soup with White Wine and Fresh Herbs

White on white … if this soup was a movie, it would be Gilda!

Serves 6

LowFatOption

Replace the olive oil with canola oil. Use low-fat vegetable stock. Replace cream with non-fat sour cream.

2 tbsp	olive oil
1	small onion, chopped
1	clove garlic, chopped
2 lb	white asparagus, cut in pieces
1	red bell pepper, chopped
5 cups	vegetable stock
1 cup	dry white wine
1/4 cup	chopped fresh basil OR 1/2 tsp dried
2 tbsp	chopped fresh oregano OR 1/4 tsp dried
2 tbsp	chopped fresh rosemary OR 1/4 tsp dried
1/2 tsp	salt
1/2 tsp	black pepper
1/2 cup	table cream
1/2 cup	finely chopped fresh parsley

Variation

Replace white asparagus with green asparagus.

In a large soup pot, heat the oil. Sauté the onion and garlic for 2 minutes. Add the asparagus and red pepper; sauté another 2 minutes. Add the stock and wine; bring to a boil and reduce to a simmer. Add the basil, oregano, rosemary, salt and black pepper. Using a hand blender, puree the soup until smooth. Stir in the cream and simmer another 2 minutes or until heated through. Stir in the parsley and serve immediately.

Artichoke and Prosciutto Soup with White Wine and Stilton

Containing cognac and stilton, this has to be the best of the best.

Serves 6

2 tbsp	unsalted butter	1/4 cup	chopped fresh parsley
4	shallots, chopped	1 tbsp	chopped fresh basil
2	cloves garlic, finely chopped	1 tbsp	chopped fresh thyme
3 cups	drained and chopped canned artichokes	1 tbsp	chopped fresh oregano
		1/2 tsp	sea salt
1	small red bell pepper, chopped	1/2 tsp	white pepper
		2 cups	table cream
1/2 cup	dry white wine	1/2 cup	chopped prosciutto
1 tbsp	cognac (optional)	1/2 cup	grated Parmesan cheese
4 cups	vegetable stock	1/4 cup	crumbled stilton

In a large soup pot, melt the butter. Add shallots and garlic; sauté for 2 minutes. Add the artichokes and red pepper; sauté another 3 minutes. Add the wine and simmer for 4 minutes. Add the cognac, stock, half of the parsley, basil, thyme, oregano, salt and white pepper; simmer for 10 minutes. Using a hand blender, puree soup until smooth. Stir in the cream, prosciutto and Parmesan. Simmer, stirring occasionally, another 5 minutes. Stir in the remaining parsley and the stilton. Serve immediately.

Avocado and Salsa Soup
with Fresh Herbs

*With this salsa soup your guests will be
tangoing up the garden path.*

Serves 6

1 tbsp	vegetable oil	1/4 cup	chopped fresh mint
1	medium red onion, chopped	1/4 cup	chopped fresh oregano
2	cloves garlic, minced	1	jalapeno pepper, chopped
1/2	green bell pepper, chopped		(optional)
1/2	red bell pepper, chopped	1 tbsp	lemon juice
4	avocados, diced	1/2 tsp	salt
1	19-oz can stewed tomatoes, diced	1/2 tsp	black pepper
		1	bay leaf
1/2 cup	chopped fresh parsley	6 cups	vegetable stock
1/2 cup	chopped fresh coriander	1/4 cup	chopped fresh chives

In a large soup pot, heat the oil. Sauté the onion and garlic for 2 minutes. Add the green pepper and red pepper; sauté for another 2 minutes. Add avocados, tomatoes and their juice, parsley, coriander, mint, oregano, jalapeno pepper, lemon juice, salt, black pepper, bay leaf and stock. Bring to a boil; reduce heat and simmer, stirring occasionally, 20 minutes. Remove the bay leaf. Garnish with chives and serve.

Low**Fat**Option
Replace the vegetable oil with 1/4 cup low-fat vegetable stock for sautéing.
216.4 cal.

Zucchini and Red Pepper Soup with Red Wine and Salsa

To make this soup extra zesty, use a hot salsa intsead of a mild one.

Serves 6

2 tbsp	olive oil
1 1/2 cups	chopped zucchini
1	red bell pepper, chopped
1	medium onion, chopped
1/2 cup	red wine
1	medium potato, peeled and cubed
1 cup	mild salsa
1/4 cup	chopped fresh basil
1 tsp	chili powder
1/2 tsp	salt
1/2 tsp	black pepper
1	bay leaf
6 cups	vegetable stock
1/4 cup	chopped fresh coriander

Variation
Add 2 sliced grilled sausages.

In a large soup pot, heat the oil. Gently sauté the zucchini, red pepper and onion for 3 minutes or until onion is translucent. Add the wine and allow to reduce for 2 minutes. Add the potato, salsa, basil, chili powder, salt, black pepper, bay leaf and stock. Bring to a boil; reduce heat and simmer for 15 minutes. Remove the bay leaf. Serve garnished with coriander.

Carrot and Orange Mint Soup

Of all my designer soups, this one is the freshest.
Enjoy it with a lovely sauterne.

Serves 6

2 tbsp	unsalted butter
6	carrots, grated (about 2 cups)
1	medium onion, chopped
1/2 tsp	grated fresh ginger
5 cups	vegetable stock
1 cup	orange juice
2 tbsp	orange zest
1/2 tsp	dried basil
1/2 tsp	chili powder
1/2 tsp	salt
1/2 tsp	white pepper
1/2 cup	chopped fresh mint
2	seedless oranges, peeled and finely chopped
1/2 cup	table cream
1/4 cup	chopped fresh parsley

In a large soup pot, melt the butter. Sauté the carrots, onion and ginger for 5 minutes. Add the stock, orange juice, orange zest, basil, chili powder, salt, pepper and half of the mint. Bring to a boil; reduce heat and simmer for 15 minutes. Add the oranges, remaining mint and cream; simmer for 5 minutes. Serve garnished with parsley.

Cream of Carrot Soup with Grand Marnier and Orange

The best way to serve carrots is with whipping cream,
table cream, tarragon and orange liqueur.
This is shockingly good.

Serves 6

3 tbsp	unsalted butter
1	medium red onion, chopped
2 1/2 cups	grated carrot
1	seedless orange, peeled and chopped
2 tbsp	Grand Marnier
2 tbsp	orange zest
5 cups	vegetable stock
1 tbsp	orange marmalade (optional)
1 tsp	dried tarragon
1/2 tsp	dried thyme
1/2 tsp	dried basil
1/2 tsp	white pepper
1/2 tsp	sea salt
1/2 cup	table cream
1/2 cup	whipping cream

In a large soup pot, melt the butter. Sauté the onion for 2 minutes. Add the carrots; sauté another 2 minutes. Add the orange, Grand Marnier and 1 tbsp of the orange zest; sauté for 2 minutes. Add the stock, marmalade, tarragon, thyme, basil, pepper and salt; simmer for 10 minutes. Using a hand blender, puree the soup until smooth. Stir in the table cream and whipping cream. Simmer another 2 minutes or until heated through and serve immediately with remaining orange zest.

Cream of Escargot Soup with Port

This is so French and oh, so good.

Serves 6

3 tbsp	unsalted butter
1	red bell pepper, chopped
4	shallots, chopped
2	cloves garlic, chopped
1 1/2 cups	chopped escargot
2 tbsp	Port
1	small potato, peeled and cubed
2 tbsp	capers
1/2 tsp	dried sage
1/2 tsp	dried basil
1/2 tsp	sea salt
1/2 tsp	white pepper
5 cups	fish stock
1 cup	table cream
1/4 cup	chopped fresh parsley

> **Variation**
>
> Replace the escargot with clams or scallops.

In a large soup pot, melt the butter. Add the red pepper, shallots and garlic; sauté for 2 minutes or until shallots are translucent. Add the escargot and sauté another 2 minutes. Add the Port and cook another 2 minutes. Add the potato, capers, sage, basil, salt, white pepper and stock; simmer 10 minutes. Stir in the cream and simmer until heated through, about 2 minutes. Garnish with parsley and serve immediately.

Cream of Shrimp Soup with Orange Liqueur

*Serve this delectable delight with jumbo shrimp
on the side.*

Serves 6

3 tbsp	unsalted butter
1	seedless orange, peeled and chopped
1	red bell pepper, chopped
4	shallots, chopped
2	cloves garlic, finely chopped
3 cups	cooked salad shrimp
1/4 cup	orange liqueur (Grand Marnier or Cointreau)
2 tbsp	orange zest
1 tbsp	chili powder
1/4 cup	chopped fresh basil
5 cups	fish stock
1 tbsp	sugar
1/2 cup	table cream
1/2 cup	whipping cream

In a large soup pot, melt the butter. Sauté the orange, red pepper, shallots and garlic for 2 to 3 minutes. Stir in the shrimp and sauté another 2 minutes. Add the orange liqueur, orange zest, chili powder and basil. Sauté for 4 minutes or until the liquid has reduced by half. Add the fish stock and sugar. Simmer for 10 minutes. Using a hand blender, puree the soup till smooth. Add the table cream and whipping cream and simmer 3 minutes or until heated through. Serve immediately.

Smoked Salmon Soup with Baby Shrimp and Vodka

Serve this with buckwheat blinis with crème fraîche and caviar.

Serves 6

2 tbsp	olive oil
2	stalks celery, finely chopped
1	small red onion, chopped
1/2	red bell pepper, finely chopped
1 cup	smoked salmon, chopped small
1 oz	vodka
6 cups	fish or vegetable stock
1/4 cup	finely chopped fresh basil
2 tbsp	chili powder
1/2 tsp	sea salt
1/2 tsp	white pepper
1 cup	cooked salad shrimp
1 cup	table cream
1/4 cup	finely chopped fresh parsley

In a large soup pot, heat the oil. Add the celery, onion and red pepper; sauté for 1 minute. Add the smoked salmon and sauté another 2 minutes. Add the vodka and sauté 2 more minutes. Add the stock, basil, chili powder, salt and white pepper. Bring to a boil; reduce heat and simmer for 15 minutes. Add the shrimp and cream. Simmer gently until heated through. Garnish with parsley and serve immediately.

Crabmeat Bisque with Dill

*One thing I will caution here: don't buy the extruded (or faux)
crab for this recipe ... stick to the real thing,
even if it is canned.*

Serves 6

2 tbsp	unsalted butter
2	stalks celery, chopped
1	small red bell pepper, chopped
4	shallots, chopped
1	medium potato, peeled and cubed
1 cup	crabmeat
1/2 cup	dry white wine
1	14-oz can stewed tomatoes, diced
1/4 cup	chopped fresh dill
1/2 tsp	dried basil
1/2 tsp	dried thyme
1/2 tsp	chili powder
1/2 tsp	salt
1/2 tsp	white pepper
1	bay leaf
5 cups	fish stock
1 cup	table cream

In a large soup pot, melt the butter. Add celery, red pepper and shallots; sauté for 3 minutes. Add potato, crabmeat and wine; simmer for 3 minutes, allowing wine to reduce. Add the tomatoes and their juice, dill, basil, thyme, chili powder, salt, pepper, bay leaf and stock. Bring to a boil; reduce heat and simmer for 15 minutes. Remove the bay leaf. Using a hand blender, puree till smooth. Stir in cream and serve immediately.

Lobster Curry Soup

Lobster with curry is an unusual,
but inspired, combination.

Serves 6

5 cups	vegetable or fish stock
2	cloves garlic, minced
1/2 cup	chopped fresh coriander
1/4 cup	chopped fresh basil
1 tbsp	mild curry powder
1 tbsp	Dijon mustard
1 tbsp	lemon juice
1/2 tsp	salt
1/2 tsp	black pepper
1	bay leaf
1 cup	canned lobster meat
1 cup	table cream
1/4 cup	chopped fresh parsley

In a large soup pot, bring the stock to a boil. Stir in the garlic, coriander, basil, curry powder, mustard, lemon juice, salt, pepper and bay leaf. Simmer for 15 minutes. Gently stir in the lobster and cream. Simmer another 5 minutes. Remove the bay leaf. Serve garnished with parsley.

Four Cheese Soup with Lobster and Fresh Herbs

*Use only freshly grated cheese in this soup,
and don't skimp on the fresh herbs.*

Serves 6

2 tbsp	unsalted butter
4	shallots, finely chopped
1	small red bell pepper, finely chopped
1 cup	cooked lobster meat
1/4 cup	dry white wine
1/4 cup	chopped fresh basil
2 tbsp	chopped fresh rosemary
2 tbsp	chopped fresh thyme
1/2 tsp	sea salt
1/2 tsp	white pepper
4 cups	fish or vegetable stock
2 cups	table cream
1/4 cup	grated gruyère cheese
1/4 cup	shredded cheddar cheese
1/4 cup	grated Parmesan cheese
1/4 cup	shredded mozzarella cheese
1/4 cup	finely chopped fresh parsley

In a large soup pot, melt the butter. Gently sauté the shallots and red pepper for
2 minutes. Add the lobster, white wine, basil, rosemary, thyme, salt and white pepper. Simmer, stirring, for 4 minutes, allowing the alcohol to burn off. Add the
stock and simmer 10 minutes. Add the cream and simmer gently until heated
through. Stir in the cheeses until melted. Serve immediately with the parsley.

Lobster Stew with Cognac and Fresh Sage

This designer soup is a star. If cognac isn't readily available, substitute armagnac, brandy or Port.

Serves 6

3 tbsp	unsalted butter
1	medium onion, chopped
1	red bell pepper, chopped
2 cups	lobster meat
1 oz	cognac
2	tomatoes, chopped
6 cups	fish stock
2 tbsp	capers
2 tbsp	finely chopped fresh sage
1 tbsp	finely chopped fresh thyme
1 tbsp	balsamic vinegar
1/2 tsp	sea salt
1/2 tsp	black pepper
1/2 cup	table cream
1/2 cup	whipping cream

Variation

Replace the lobster with 2 cubed, cooked monkfish steaks.

In a large soup pot, melt the butter. Sauté the onion and red bell pepper for 2 minutes. Add the lobster meat and sauté another 2 minutes. Add cognac; sauté another 4 minutes, allowing the liquid to reduce by half. Add the tomatoes, stock, capers, sage, thyme, balsamic vinegar, salt and black pepper; simmer for 10 minutes. Stir in the table cream and whipping cream and heat gently until heated through. Serve immediately.

Steak and Lobster Soup with Red Wine and Fresh Herbs

*This surf and turf extravaganza, with salad
and freshly baked bread, is all you need!*

Serves 6

2 tbsp	unsalted butter
1	red bell pepper, chopped
4	shallots, chopped
2	cloves garlic, chopped
1/2 cup	lobster meat
1/2 cup	red wine
1	28-oz can stewed tomatoes, diced
1/4 cup	chopped fresh basil
1 tbsp	chopped fresh rosemary
1/2 tsp	sea salt
1/2 tsp	black pepper
1	bay leaf
3 cups	fish stock
3 cups	beef stock
1	6-oz New York steak, grilled and thinly sliced
1	lobster tail, grilled and thinly sliced
1/4 cup	chopped fresh parsley

> **Variation**
> Replace the lobster meat with crabmeat.

In a large soup pot, melt the butter. Add red pepper, shallots and garlic; sauté for 2 minutes or until the shallots are translucent. Add the lobster and sauté another 2 minutes. Add the wine and simmer for 4 minutes or until the wine has reduced by half. Add the stewed tomatoes and their juice, basil, rosemary, salt, black pepper, bay leaf and stocks; simmer for 10 minutes. Add the steak and sliced lobster tail. Simmer another 5 minutes. Remove the bay leaf. Serve garnished with parsley.

Mussel Soup with Coconut Milk and Pernod

The flavours of coconut milk and Pernod
will make you swoon (it's so good)!

Serves 6

3 tbsp	unsalted butter
1	red bell pepper, chopped
6	shallots, chopped
2	cloves garlic, chopped
1 oz	Pernod
4 cups	fish stock
1/4 cup	chopped fresh basil
1 tbsp	chopped fresh thyme
1 tbsp	Dijon mustard
1/2 tsp	sea salt
1/2 tsp	black pepper
1 cup	unsweetened coconut milk
1 cup	table cream
1 1/2 lb	mussels, cleaned
1/4 cup	shaved fresh OR unsweetened flaked coconut
1/4 cup	chopped fresh parsley

In a large soup pot, melt the butter. Sauté the red pepper, shallots and garlic for 2 minutes. Add the Pernod and sauté another 2 minutes, allowing the alcohol to burn off. Add the stock, basil, thyme, mustard, salt and black pepper; simmer for 8 minutes. Stir in the coconut milk and cream. Raise the heat and add the mussels. Cover and simmer 4 to 5 minutes or until the mussels open. (Discard any mussels that do not open.) Serve garnished with shaved coconut and parsley.

Frogs' Leg Soup with White Wine and Fresh Rosemary

Don't even think of substituting toads' legs for frogs'!

Serves 6

7 cups	fish stock	1/2 cup	dry white wine
8	frogs' legs	2 tbsp	finely chopped fresh
3 tbsp	unsalted butter		rosemary
2	stalks celery, chopped	1 tbsp	chopped fresh thyme
2	medium carrots, grated	1 tbsp	Dijon mustard
1	small green bell pepper,	1 tbsp	balsamic vinegar
	finely chopped	1/2 tsp	sea salt
6	shallots, finely chopped	1/2 tsp	white pepper
2	cloves garlic, finely chopped	1	bay leaf

In a large soup pot, combine the stock and frogs' legs. Bring to a boil; reduce heat and simmer for 10 minutes. Remove frogs' legs and take all the meat off the bones. Discard the bones and set aside the meat. In a sauté pan, melt the butter. Sauté the celery, carrots, green pepper, shallots and garlic for 3 minutes. Add the wine and sauté until the liquid is reduced by half. Empty the shallot mixture into the fish stock. Add the rosemary, thyme, mustard, balsamic vinegar, salt, white pepper and bay leaf. Simmer for 5 minutes. Add the frogs' legs meat; simmer for another 3 to 4 minutes or until heated through. Remove the bay leaf and serve immediately.

Index

Apple
    bacon and cabbage, 157
    and beef cinnamon soup, 146
    and carrot soup, 19
    and curried pork soup, 159
    and parsnip soup, 69
    and pear soup, chilled, 78
    and pumpkin soup, 59
    and sweet potato soup, 13
    soup, chilled, 79

Artichoke and Asparagus Soup with White Wine, 61

Artichoke and Prosciutto Soup with White Wine and Stilton, 171

Artichoke soups
    and asparagus, 61
    cream of, 28
    and prosciutto, 171

Asparagus soups
    artichoke and, 61
    cream of, 23
    with white wine and herbs, 170

Avocado and Fresh Mint Soup, 35

Avocado and Salsa Soup with Fresh Herbs, 172

Avocado soups
    and mint, 35
    and pear, chilled, 77
    and salsa, 172

Baby Shrimp Tomato Soup, 120

Bacon
    cabbage and apple soup, 157
    celery and tomato soup, 156
    and chick pea soup, 155
    and potato cheese soup, 44
    white bean and potato soup, 44

Bacon and Chick Pea Soup with Herbs, 155

Bacon and Potato Cheese Soup, 154

Bacon, Cabbage and Apple Soup, 157

Bacon, Celery and Spicy Tomato Soup, 156

Barley
    and beef soup, 147
    mushroom and pork, 158

Bean soups
    black, with corn, 49
    with cheddar and ham, 46
    chicken and, 128
    creamy mixed, 39
    mushroom and chili, 45
    with potato and bacon, 44
    potato puree, 41
    with sausage, 47
    shrimp and salsa, 40
    spicy black, 48
    tomato, 42
    vegetable, 38
    white, and chick pea, 43

Beef and Apple Cinnamon Soup, 146

Beef and Curry Soup with Yogurt, 100

Beef Barley Soup with Red Wine and Roasted Garlic, 147

Beef soups
    and apple, 146
    barley soup, 147
    and curry, 100
    and egg noodle, 148
    hamburger and chili, 101
    hamburger and Parmesan, 150
    meatball and egg noodle, 149
    pepperpot with blue cheese, 151
    spicy, with salsa and sun-dried tomato, 152
    steak and lobster, 183
    steak and vegetable, 153

Beef Stock, 5

Beet soups
    Chilled Borscht with Sour Cream, 74
    with Red Pepper and Roasted Garlic, 59

Bell pepper soup, spicy, 60

Black Bean Salsa Soup with Corn, 49

Blue Cheese Celery Soup, 169

Borscht, chilled, 74

Broccoli soup, cream of, 24

Broth, chicken with ginger and coriander, 4

Butternut Squash Soup, Curried, 15

Butternut Squash Soup with Curry and Apple, 94

Cabbage soup, bacon and apple, 157

Carrot and Apple Soup with Ginger, 19

Carrot and Ginger Mint Soup, 89

Carrot and Orange Mint Soup, 174

Carrot soups
and apple, 19
and ginger, 89
with Grand Marnier and orange, 175
and orange, 174
potato and leek, 68

Carrot, Potato and Leek Soup with
Mint, 68

Cauliflower and Mushroom Soup, 17

Cauliflower soups
celery and, 62
and mushroom, 17
potato and, 93

Celery and Cauliflower Soup with White
Wine, 62

Celery and Potato Soup with Feta and
Rosemary, 92

Celery soups
bacon and tomato, 156
blue cheese, 169
and cauliflower, 62
potato, 64
and potato, with feta, 92

Chick pea
and bacon soup, 155
and white bean soup, 43

Chicken, Bean and Coriander Soup, 128

Chicken and Lime Soup, 133

Chicken and Macaroni Soup with Salsa,
98

Chicken and Rice Soup with Spinach
and White Wine, 99

Chicken Broth with Ginger and
Coriander, 4

Chicken Coconut Soup with
Lemongrass and Fennel, 136

Chicken Monterey Jack Soup with
Salsa, 129

Chicken Soup with Portobello
Mushrooms and Red Wine, 127

Chicken soups
bean and coriander, 128
and coconut milk, 135
coconut, 136
cream of, 131
curried, with apple, 137
eastern with raisins and rosemary, 140
egg drop, 130
with ginger, 4
hot and sour, 132
lemon with leek, 134
and lime, 133
and macaroni, 98
and Monterey Jack, 129
Mulligatawny, 138
with mushrooms, 127
oriental, 139
with rice, 99, 126
and sausage, 162

Chicken stock, 2, 3

Chilled soups
Chilled Apple Cinnamon Soup, 79
Chilled Apple and Pear Soup, 78
Chilled Avocado and Pear Soup, 76
Chilled Borscht with Sour Cream, 74
Chilled Cucumber Mint Soup, 76
Chilled Honeydew Melon Soup with
Cinnamon, 82
Chilled Peach Soup with Parsley, 80
Chilled Pineapple and Coconut
Soup, 83
Chilled Strawberry Mint Soup, 81

Cool Fennel Soup, 75
Cool Vegetable Soup with Herbs, 88
Gazpacho, 72
Way Down South Gazpacho, 73

Chowders
clam, low-fat, 96
corn and potato, 30
creamy clam, 114
Creole conch, 112
Mediterranean fish, 105
quick fish, 110
salmon, 111
tomato clam, 115
turkey, 97

Clam Chowder, low-fat, 96

Clam soups
creamy chowder, 114
tomato clam, 115
traditional no-cream, 113

Coconut, and pineapple soup, chilled, 83

Cold soups *See* Chilled soups

Cool Fennel Soup, 75

Cool Vegetable Soup with Herbs, 88

Corn and Potato Chowder with
Cheese, 30

Corn and Potato Soup, 65

Corn chowder, and potato, 30

Corn soups
chowder, 30
and potato, 29
oriental chicken and, 139
with rosemary and port, 31

Corn Soup with Rosemary and Port, 31

Crabmeat Bisque with Dill, 179

Cream of Artichoke Soup, 28

Cream of Asparagus Soup with Roasted
Garlic and Basil, 23

Cream of Broccoli and Cheese Soup, 24

Cream of Carrot Soup with Grand Marnier and Orange, 175

Cream of Chicken Soup with Sage, 131

Cream of Corn and Potato Soup, 29

Cream of Escargot Soup with Port, 176

Cream of Garlic Soup with Capers, 166

Cream of Leek Soup with Chives and Sour Cream, 27

Cream of Mushroom Soup, 22

Cream of Shrimp Soup with Orange Liqueur, 177

Cream of Zucchini and Herb Soup, 25

Cream of Zucchini Soup with Tarragon, 26

Creamy Beef and Egg Noodle Soup, 148

Creamy Clam Chowder, 114

Creamy Mixed Bean Soup, 39

Creamy Spinach Soup with Fennel, 12

Creole Conch Chowder, 112

Cucumber soup, chilled, 76

Curried Butternut Squash Soup, 15

Curried Chicken Soup with Apple, 137

Curried Pork Soup with Apple and Chutney, 159

Eastern Chicken Soup with Raisins and Rosemary, 140

Egg Drop Soup with Chicken and Soup, 130

Eggplant, zucchini and red pepper, 57

Escargot soup, 176

Fennel soup
    cool, 75
    and spinach, 12

Fish Soup Italian-Style, 106

Fish Soup with Pineapple and Coconut, 107

Fish Stock, 6, 7

Four Cheese Soup with Lobster and Fresh Herbs, 181

French onion soup, 54

Frogs' Leg Soup with White Wine and Fresh Rosemary, 185

Garlic soup
    with capers, 166
    roasted, and wild rice, 167

Gazpacho, 72
    Way Down South, 73

Grilled Beef Steak and Vegetable Soup, 153

Grilled Chicken and Coconut Milk Soup, 135

Grilled Shrimp and Vegetable Chili Soup, 119

Grilled Vegetable Soup with Fresh Herbs, 53

Hamburger and Chili Soup, 101

Hamburger and Parmesan Soup, 150

Homey Chicken Soup with Rice, 126

Honeydew soup, chilled, 82

Hot and Sour Grilled Chicken Soup, 132

Ken's French Onion Soup, 54

Kenny's Chicken Stock, 2

Kenny's Fancy Fish Stock, 7

Kenny's Special Vegetable Stock, 9

Kidney Bean Soup with Cheddar and Ham, 46

Lamb, Apricot and Ginger Soup, 161

Lamb, Feta and Rosemary Rice Soup, 160

Leek soups
    carrot and potato, 68
    cream of, 27
    lemon chicken, 134
    potato and, 33

Lemon Chicken Soup with Leek, 134

Lentil soups
    and tomato, 18
    with lemon and parsley, 56

Lobster Curry Soup, 180

Lobster Stew with Cognac and Fresh Sage, 182

Lots of Mushroom Soup, 21

Low-Fat Chicken Stock, 3

Low-fat soups
    Beef and Curry Soup with Yogurt, 100
    Butternut Squash Soup with Curry and Apple, 94
    Carrot and Ginger Mint Soup, 89
    Celery and Potato Soup with Feta and Rosemary, 92
    Chicken and Macaroni Soup with Salsa, 98
    Chicken and Rice Soup with Spinach and White Wine, 99
    Clam Chowder, 96

Cool Vegetable Soup with Herbs, 88
Hamburger and Chili Soup, 101
Low-Fat Minestrone with Fresh Sage, 86
Mushroom and Pasta Soup with Black Forest Ham, 90
Potato and Cauliflower Soup with Coriander, 93
Quick-and-Easy Vegetable Soup with Fresh Herbs and Red Wine, 87
Simple Mushroom Soup with Potato and Sour Cream, 91
Spicy Tomato and Seafood Soup, 95
Turkey Chowder, 97

Macaroni, and chicken soup, 98

Mashed Potato Delight with Roasted Garlic and Cheese, 67

Meatball and Parmesan Egg Noodle Soup, 149

Mediterranean Fish Chowder with Red Wine and Herbs, 105

Melon soup, chilled, 82

Mixed Bean Shrimp and Salsa Soup, 40

Mixed Mushroom Soup with Fresh Herbs, 55

Mulligatawny, 138

Mushroom and Pasta Soup with Black Forest Ham, 90

Mushroom soup, 21
  barley and pork, 158
  bean and chili, 45
  and cauliflower, 17
  cream of, 22
  mixed, with herbs, 55
  portobello and chicken soup, 127
  with potato and sour cream, 91
  spicy, 20

Mussel Soup with Coconut Milk and Pernod, 184

Mussel Soup with Garlic and Coriander, 118

Mussel Soup with Lemon and Tarragon, 117

Mussel Tomato Soup with Basil, 116

Onion soups
  Ken's French, 54
  with white wine and coriander, 168

Orange, and carrot mint soup, 174

Oriental Chicken and Corn Soup, 139

Parsnip and Apple Soup with Maple Syrup, 69

Pasta soups
  macaroni and chicken, 98
  and mushroom, 90

Pea soup, and sausage, 163

Peach soup, chilled, 80

Pear
  and apple soup, chilled, 78
  and avocado soup, chilled, 77

Pearl Onion Soup with White Wine and Coriander, 68

Pepperpot with Blue Cheese, 151

Peppers See Bell pepper; Red pepper

Pesto Potato Soup with White Wine, 63

Pineapple, and coconut soup, chilled, 83

Pork
  curried soup with apple and chutney, 159
  mushroom and barley soup, 158

Portobello Mushroom, Barley and Grilled Pork Soup, 158

Potato and Cauliflower Soup with Coriander, 93

Potato and Celery Soup with Herbs, 64

Potato and Leek Soup with White Wine and Tarragon, 33

Potato chowder and corn, 30

Potato soups
  bacon and cheese, 154
  bean and bacon, 44
  carrot and leek, 68
  and cauliflower, 93
  celery and, 64, 92
  and corn, 29, 65
  with garlic and cheese, 67
  and leek, 33
  pesto, 63

Pumpkin Curry Soup, 16

Pumpkin Soup with Apple and Cinnamon, 58

Quick Fish Chowder with Herbs, 110

Quick-and-Easy Turkey Wild Rice Soup, 143

Red Bean Soup with Sausage, 47

Red Bean, Mushroom and Chili Soup, 45

Red pepper soup, 34
  beet and roasted garlic, 59
  zucchini and, 173
  zucchini and eggplant, 57

Red snapper and sole soup, 104

Rice, and chicken soup, 99

Roasted Garlic with Wild Rice Soup with Fresh Basil, 167

Salmon Chowder, 111

Sausage and Chicken Gumbo, 162

Sausage Split Pea Soup with Dijon, 163

Scallop Soup with Red Wine and Rosemary, 121

Seafood soups
  Baby Shrimp Tomato Soup, 120
  bean, shrimp and salsa, 40
  clam chowder, 96
  clam, low-fat, 96
  crabmeat bisque, 179
  Creamy Clam Chowder, 114
  Creole Conch Chowder, 112
  Fish Soup Italian-Style, 106
  Fish Soup with Pineapple and Coconut, 107
  fish stock, 6, 7
  four cheese with lobster, 181
  Grilled Shrimp and Vegetable Chili Soup, 119
  lobster curry soup, 180
  lobster stew, 182
  Mediterranean Fish Chowder with Red Wine and Herbs, 105
  mussel soup, 184
  Mussel Soup with Garlic and Coriander, 118
  Mussel Soup with Lemon and Tarragon, 117
  Mussel Tomato Soup with Basil, 116
  Quick Fish Chowder with Herbs, 110
  Salmon Chowder, 111
  Scallop Soup with Red Wine and Rosemary, 121
  smoked salmon and baby shrimp, 178
  Sole and Red Snapper Soup with White Wine and Apple, 104

Squid Soup with Roasted Garlic and Sage, 122
  steak and lobster, 183
  Swordfish Soup with Coconut Milk and Rum, 108
  Swordfish Soup with Parsley and Lime, 109
  Tangy Tomato Clam Chowder, 115
  Traditional No-Cream Clam Soup, 113
Shrimp soups
  bean and salsa, 40
  grilled, and vegetable chili, 119
  with orange liqueur, 177
  and tomato, 120
Simple Mushroom Soup with Potato and Sour Cream, 91
Smoked Salmon Soup with Baby Shrimp and Vodka, 178
Sole and Red Snapper Soup with White Wine and Apple, 104
Spicy Beef Soup with Salsa and Sun-Dried Tomato, 152
Spicy Black Bean Soup, 48
Spicy Mixed Bean Potato Puree with Cheddar Cheese, 41
Spicy Mixed Bell Pepper Soup with Red Wine, 60
Spicy Mushroom Soup with Cheese, 20
Spicy Red Pepper Soup with Fresh Parsley, 34
Spicy Tomato and Seafood Soup, 95
Spicy Tomato White Bean Soup with Red Wine, 42
Spicy Vegetable Soup, 52
Spinach soups
  butternut, 15, 94

with fennel, 12
Squid Soup with Roasted Garlic and Sage, 122
Steak and Lobster Soup with Red Wine and Fresh Herbs, 183
Stock
  beef, 5
  chicken, 2, 3
  fish, 6, 7
  vegetable, 8, 9
Strawberry soup, chilled, 81
Sweet Potato Soup with Apple and Cinnamon, 13
Sweet Potato Soup with Curry and Nutmeg, 14
Swordfish Soup with Coconut Milk and Rum, 108
Swordfish Soup with Parsley and Lime, 109

Tangy Tomato Clam Chowder, 115
Tomato soups
  baby shrimp, 120
  and lentil, 18
  mussel, 116
  spicy, and seafood, 95
  tangy clam chowder, 115
  white bean, 42
Traditional No-Cream Clam Soup, 113
True Potato Soup with Parmesan, 32
Turkey Chowder, 97
Turkey soups
  chowder, 97
  easy chili, 142
  quick and easy wild rice, 143
  with salsa, 141

Turkey Soup with Salsa and Mint, 141

Vegetable stock, 8, 9

Vegetable Bean Soup with a Load of
Basil, 38

Vegetable soups
  bacon, cabbage and apple, 157
  bacon, celery and tomato, 156
  bean, 38
  grilled shrimp, 119

grilled, with herbs, 53
spicy, 52

Very Easy Turkey Chili Soup, 142

Way Down South Gazpacho, 73

White Asparagus Soup with White Wine
and Fresh Herbs, 170

White Bean and Chick Pea Puree, 43

White Bean Soup with Potato and

Bacon, 44

Zesty Zucchini, Eggplant and Red
Pepper Soup, 57

Zucchini and Red Pepper Soup with Red
Wine and Salsa, 173

Zucchini soup
  cream of, 25, 26
  eggplant and red pepper, 57
  and red pepper, 173

Dear Ken

If you'd like to write to Ken to provide feedback or to relate your culinary adventures, please address your letters to:

Ken Kostick
Box 116
2255 Queen Street East
Toronto, Ontario
M4E 1G3

About Ken, Pearl & Benny

Born in Winnipeg, Toronto-based Ken Kostick has had a varied career in travel and fashion, including the creation of his own modeling agency. Before becoming a full-time cooking show host and cookbook author, Ken logged thousands of miles each year as an international model scout, searching for the "next" supermodel.

Always looking for new challenges, Ken is also pursuing acting in television and musical theatre and recently performed in a production of *Crazy For You* at the Rainbow Stage. Not surprising, then, is this little-known fact about Ken: he smokes up the dance floor when he dons his tap shoes.

Currently, Ken divides his time between Toronto, Lake Winnipeg, and South Beach, Florida.

Pearl, bred in Ontario and raised in Toronto, has been a popular guest on *What's for Dinner?* since her infancy, delighting guests with her gambolling gait, generous jowls, and deadpan stare. Elegant and dainty, Pearl's a natural on camera; off camera, she's been known to swipe the odd sandwich or petit fours. Slavishly devoted to Ken, and very good-natured all-round, she "tolerates" Benny.

Big, lumbering, adorable Benny was found in a pet shop in Winnipeg, Manitoba. Once quite small, he has grown to almost freakish proportions; his girth makes it difficult for him to climb stairs and he often needs help to lift his back-end on to the couch (or just about anything elevated). Almost beyond reproach, Benny will occasionally bark at neighbours, uninvited guests or long skirts. Benny admires Pearl.